THIRTEEN MONTHS

THIRTEEN MONTHS

ONE MARINE'S MEMOIR

AS TOLD TO C.E. MARR

Palmetto Publishing Group
Charleston, SC

Thirteen Months: One Marine's Memoir
Copyright © 2018 by C.E. Marr
All rights reserved

First Edition

Printed in the United States

ISBN-13: 978-1-64111-183-6
ISBN-10: 1-64111-183-6

For Jim
James, Mary, and Jean

ACKNOWLEDGEMENTS

Thanks to Crystal Klimavicz, without whose expertise this book would not have been possible.

Thanks to Carol Padgett for her sharp eye in lending grammatical assistance and to Barb Fabey for multiple readings of the text.

Thanks to Kenneth Padgett for his excellent graphic design for the maps and book cover.

Special thanks to Lt. Col. Jim Amendolia, USMC, Ret., Col. Frank Wilbourne, USMC, Ret. and Mr. Dave Pitchford, for their helpful critiques and encouragement.

BREAKDOWN OF US MARINE RANK STRUCTURE

A squad is comprised of fourteen men. Usually the squad leader is a Sergeant, who is an enlisted man, commonly referred to as non-commissioned officer, or NCO. This rank is above Private, Private First Class, Lance Corporal, Corporal, or Sergeant, E-5.

Three squads make up a platoon. A platoon is led by a Second Lieutenant.

Four platoons make a company. A company is commanded by a Captain. Each company also has an executive officer, usually a first lieutenant.

Five companies make a battalion. battalions are generally commanded by a lieutenant colonel with two majors as staff officers under the Lieutenant Colonel's command.

Three battalions make up a regiment. regiments are commanded by a Colonel, with two majors as staff officers under the colonel's command.

Three regiments make a division. The Marine Corps has three divisions. The Marine Corps has three active divisions and one reserve division. Each division is commanded by a Major General.

USMC RANKS AND INSIGNIAS

ENLISTED MEN

Private: E-1 (*E* stands for "enlisted"); no insignia or stripe

Private First Class: E-2; one stripe

Lance Corporal: E-3; one stripe over crossed rifles

Corporal: E -4; two stripes over crossed rifles

Sergeant: E-5; three stripes over crossed rifles

Staff Sergeant: E-6; three stripes up and one stripe down, with crossed rifles in middle

Gunnery Sergeant: E-7; three stripes up, two stripes down, with crossed rifles in middle

First Sergeant: E-8; three stripes up, three stripes down, with diamond in middle

Sergeant Major: E-9; three stripes up, four stripes down, with Marine Corps emblem in the middle with star on either side

Sergeant Major of the Marine Corps: E-9; three stripes up, four stripes down, with Marine Corps emblem in the middle with one star on each side.

WARRANT OFFICERS

W-1: gold bar with two red squares

W-2: gold bar with thee red squares

W-3: silver bar with two blue squares

W-4: silver bar with three blue squares

OFFICERS (OUTRANK ALL ENLISTED MEN)

Second Lieutenant: O1 (*O* stands for "officer"); gold bar insignia

First Lieutenant: O2; silver bar

Captain: O3; two silver bars (sometimes called "railroad tracks")

Major: O4; gold oak leaf

Lieutenant Colonel: O5; silver oak leaf

Colonel: O6; silver eagle

Brigadier General: O7; one star

Major General: O8; two stars

Lieutenant General: O9; three stars

General, Commandant of the Marine Corps: O10; four stars (During the Vietnam War, there was only one four-star general.)

PREFACE

When World War II came to an end, colonialism worldwide was also coming to a troubled end. Vietnam was one of those countries that survived the World War, but struggled to find independence from generations of European domination by France. The Vietnamese fought continuously after World War II against the French Army. The main event dividing the country was the Battle of Dien Bien Phu in 1954, when Vietnamese forces defeated the French.

After the French departed, the Asian country of Vietnam was divided between predominately Catholics and some Buddhists in the south, while the north remained mostly Buddhist and other varying forms of Asian religions. The split between north and south was triggered by the Catholic migration to the south, as well as remnants of Vietnamese citizens affiliated with colonialism. The migration was in opposition to the secularist Communists who then took over the north. The north aligned with China and Russia in their political beliefs. The south aligned with France and the United States.

The US was asked but steadfastly refused to intervene in helping the French retain colonialist power. The split between north and south geographically was divided by the demilitarized zone (DMZ), yet the divisions among the people themselves varied in different sections of the country between north and south.

During that same year of 1954, the US sent military assistance and advisors to the South Vietnamese. Ten years later, in August

1964, the North Vietnamese attacked a US Naval vessel in international waters off the coast of Vietnam, known as the Gulf of Tonkin incident. Subsequently, tensions ran high, and by 1965, US President Lyndon B. Johnson ordered US troops to intervene in defense of South Vietnam to avoid "communist aggression" from the north invading the south.

The Ben Hai River was the dividing line between North and South Vietnam. The area three miles north of the river and three miles south was to be the demilitarized zone (DMZ). By international agreement, all military forces were required to stay away from the DMZ. It was not to be used for military operations or bases. US troops were not allowed to fire into the DMZ, even if fired upon.

The United States Marines landed at both Da Nang and Chu Lai in the northern part of South Vietnam in the spring of 1965.

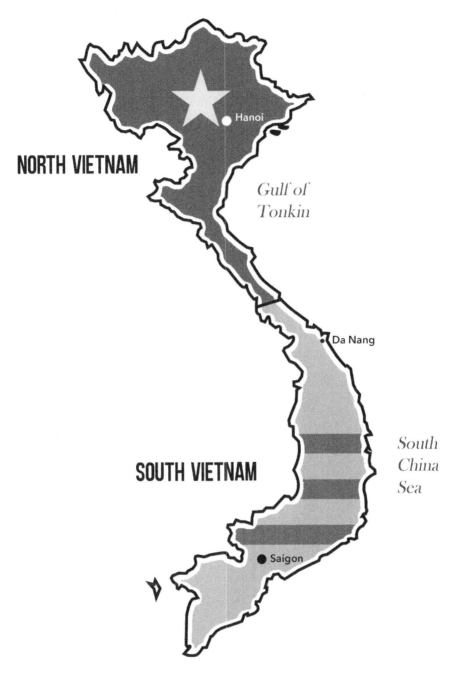

—

INTRODUCTION

It is estimated during the period 1964 to 1975, anywhere from fifty-six- to fifty-eight thousand US servicemen and servicewomen lost their lives in Vietnam. Of that number, many served in the United States Marine Corps.

The following is a true story of what life was like for one junior Marine officer during the time he fought in the Vietnam War at the DMZ. It chronicles the approximately thirteen-month period in the life of a lieutenant from the end of December 1966 to the end of January 1968.

Many books, articles, and websites about the Vietnam War have included technical details of battles and statistics from that time period. This memoir attempts to provide not only a correct timeline, but also to tell firsthand how one Marine thought and felt.

The main character—the Lieutenant—is purposely not named for the simple truth that he could be any one of the thousands of Marines who served. Decades later, the Lieutenant's recollections are sharp and his account represents what truths and beliefs Marines have always stood for: duty, integrity, loyalty, and love of country. In some instances, where dialogue has been inserted, the source assured that the story accurately portrays events as they happened.

Recognizably, another Marine could tell this story differently. During the same period, there were those who perhaps suffered more serious wounds, or underwent worse combat conditions,

displayed more or less heroism, or other factors. For this book, the words remain true to one man's story while saluting all those Marines who have gone before and after him, living or deceased, who have boldly, courageously, and proudly served in the United States Marine Corps.

CHAPTER 1

ARRIVAL AT CHU LAI

FEBRUARY 16, 1967
DAY ONE

The Marine Lieutenant was just twenty-two years old when he first found himself in combat. Days earlier, he'd sailed aboard the USS *Iwo Jima* alongside two other ships. They departed from Okinawa and headed down the Western Pacific to the South China Sea. The three ships stopped at Mindoro Island in the Philippines to allow the shipboard troops to practice one last amphibious landing before arriving in Vietnam. Once there, the ships rested in the choppy waters south of Chu Lai on the east coast of South Vietnam, well below the demilitarized zone (DMZ), but still in the Northern or I Corps sector of the country.

From the ship's flight deck, twenty-four 1950s vintage UH-34 helicopters ferried Alpha Company, about 250 men, to a spot a few miles inland. Since UH-34's could only carry four or five men at a time, the task took most of the morning. Under an already scorching sun, the Lieutenant's platoon, the Weapon's Platoon, one of four platoons that made up Alpha Company, gathered to await the start of the military operation.

Simultaneously, about twenty amphibious tractors (amtracs) rolled out of a sister ship's belly and then onto the beach just south of Chu Lai. The date was February 16, 1967.

The Lieutenant stood and waited for the last of his platoon to join the Marines already ashore. Most of the Marines under his command were still teenagers. One or two were just seventeen. He felt a heavy responsibility for their well being. Under his command were four sergeants; eight corporals (squad leaders); and fifty-four lance corporals, privates first class, or privates—sixty-six men in all. They were his priority and he knew each man by name.

The Lieutenant tended toward an introverted personality. He was serious and somewhat of a loner, yet he possessed the self-esteem to take charge whenever a situation called for action. At an even six feet tall, he carried himself with the sure confidence instilled in him through his rigorous Marine training. Fair haired, slender, and muscular, his perfect Roman nose and chiseled good looks seemed to have escaped his consciousness. He bore not a trace of conceit over his appearance, one only slightly marred by a thin, faded scar at the corner of his right eye. He also carried a smaller vertical scar dead center on his forehead. Both were souvenirs from neighborhood altercations during his hardscrabble youth. A shy smile revealed a slightly chipped front tooth, the ever-present reminder of a rock fight at age ten.

Like the others, the Lieutenant wore an olive-drab utility uniform and sleeveless flak jacket. His ice-blue eyes peered out from under his combat helmet in an earnest, almost innocent way, as he scanned the scrubby landscape before him contemplating the upcoming campaign, Operation Deckhouse VI. The new officer felt uneasy wondering about his first war experience.

Will I do the right thing under fire? Will it be anything like our training? I've seen dozens of war movies since I was a kid; now, I wonder what combat will really be like.

He watched as the choppers finished transporting the last members of Alpha Company to the landing zone. The men assembled into individual platoons. The Lieutenant's men, the Weapons Platoon, sought immediate cover in the vicinity of the nearby shrubs and trees, as they would do at any landing zone. The reason was simple: Any helicopter action generally precipitated random enemy gunfire. The Marines remained at the ready and listened for their next command.

With a hand on his hip, the Lieutenant snapped the first order to his men.

"Listen up! We're headed to a village just north of here. Keep in wedge formation from left to right. First and Third Squads, you provide flank security. Our objective: Find and destroy North Vietnamese hidden caches of arms, equipment and food supplies. When you find those things, the engineers attached to Alpha Company will then blow 'em up. Saddle up and move out!"

The platoon, well trained and eager for combat, knew instinctively what to do. Tense with anticipation, the men slung their weapons, M14 rifles, 60mm mortars, M60 machine guns, or 3.5-inch rocket launchers, over their shoulders. Silently they began the slow trudge north.

Theoretically, the Lieutenant felt as if this operation was preventative. He thought they were not particularly effective, because the operations like this one only provided a temporary solution to a long-term problem. The enemy could restock and rebuild as soon as the Marines left the area. But no one had asked his opinion and he had to follow orders. From his training, he believed "search and destroy" missions were generally a waste of time.

The troops spread out. They swept through terrain thick with shrubs, bushes, and abundant rice paddies. Hot and stinking, the rice paddies were shin high with putrid water. Around them, flies buzzed in thick swarms over water buffalo feces, which littered the paddies and made the men feel as though they were wading through open-air sewers. Steam rose from the water, evaporating in the intense morning heat, leaving a repugnant stench in the moist air.

After maneuvering in a combat wedge formation for approximately two miles, volleys of bullets from a camouflaged enemy bunker flew directly at the surprised men. No one had heard them coming. Everyone dove for cover. The Lieutenant felt this stomach knot and his throat tighten. As he directed his first firefight he hoped his men wouldn't hear the tentativeness in his voice. Down on one knee, the Lieutenant shouted, "Incoming from right front! All squads return fire! Direct your machine gunfire to right front and hold the mortars and rockets!"

The platoon returned fire. After a few minutes, the gunfire subsided. Miraculously, no one was hit. Sniper fire—maybe four or five shooting at them, but thankfully, no Leatherneck causalities. Most likely the shooters ran off as soon as they encountered return fire.

Those NVA bastards are lousy shots, the Lieutenant thought to himself.

The platoon moved on. By evening, they had covered five slow and tedious miles. Their early morning eagerness and the day's tension had turned to fatigue. At dark, the Lieutenant commanded his weary troops,

"Stop, dig in! Platoon sergeant, set up a perimeter defense!"

A perimeter defense was akin to "circling the wagons" from the pioneer days when homesteaders were under Indian attack. The human circle provided defensive coverage from any direction. Men formed a large circle around their encampment to remain vigilant against the NVA during the night hours. The Lieutenant directed the positioning of the M60 machine guns to cover all dead spaces and ensure interlocking bands of fire to defend the perimeter.

Away from rice patties, on solid ground, the company formed a defensive circle with each platoon in different arcs around it. They dug two-man foxholes, each hole about three feet deep. Immediately, the Lieutenant assigned about fifteen Marines from his platoon to nearby areas to guard any location where their platoon could possibly be attacked. Each team took a four-hour shift.

Other men were posted on alert-shifts, listening and looking for the enemy throughout the night. Listen for four hours; rest for four. The others ate and tried to sleep before their turn came.

Food in the field was strictly C-rations. Each man carried a cardboard box of them in his backpack. C's contained a small can filled with tasteless white bread about the size of a little coffee mug; a packet of cheese or peanut butter; another miniature tin of fruit or fruit cocktail; four cigarettes; matches; and a plastic spoon. Also included in each box was a small can opener that most men attached to their dog tags with a string.

The men drank fetid water from the paddies, using iodine tablets for purification. Each man would put two or three pills in his water canteen. The tablets were also intended to kill water parasites. The tiny pills gave the water a pungent, acrid smell, with the medicinal taste of iodine, like drinking rubbing alcohol.

The Lieutenant overheard a private grumble to another Marine as he walked by, "First they starve us with these damn C's, and then all we get to drink is this shitty water. Wouldn't mind a cold beer about now."

The Lieutenant agreed, but he held his silence, pretending not to hear. Because of the extreme heat and humidity, the Lieutenant issued the order while his platoon was eating their C's: "Men, in addition to the iodine tablets in your water, be sure you swallow at least six salt pills every twenty-four hours. These will keep you from getting dehydration, heat stroke, heat exhaustion, or heat cramps."

More grumbling. (But those who didn't obey would suffer severe stomach and muscle cramps.)

That night sleep was impossible. Sporadic sniper fire, random incoming mortars, and the occasional sound of grenades exploding in the distance broke through the night until dusk the next morning. Everyone remained vigilant. The Lieutenant never closed his eyes.

FEBRUARY 17, 1967
DAY TWO

When morning came with no sign of the enemy, the platoon continued heading north as part of A Company's formation. Already wet from a morning rain shower, the men slogged through more rank rice paddies. The Lieutenant and his men itched all over from bug bites, mosquitoes mostly, he guessed. The no-brand repellent they carried in small plastic bottles in their packs had already proven ineffective.

To add to his own discomfort, the Lieutenant's boots had filled with paddy water. Although he wore heavy socks, multiple blisters had formed on his feet. There was no way to dry his feet and no relief. The platoon trudged on.

During a mid-day break, the tired Lieutenant reflected for a moment on the realization that he was no longer participating in a training exercise. This was the real thing. He knew it, too, by the grisly scene his platoon had stumbled upon earlier that morning. An American-made Claymore mine had picked off a North Vietnamese soldier, leaving only a hand and twenty meters of rotting intestine in a pool of blood. Nearby lay another uniformed North Vietnamese body missing the back of his skull. His bloody brains spilled out on the ground. They dried up in the intense heat, like a broken dark-amber jar of baked beans. So vivid was the image imprinted on the Lieutenant's mind that he vowed to himself never to eat baked beans again. Disgusted at the sight, he wondered who might be next to suffer dismemberment or death.

Claymore mines were ten inches wide and five inches high. They were put in place with a wire camouflaged with sand or leaves and attached to a mine. Then the wire was extended back to where the ambush or defensive position was being set up, similar to how dynamite is set. Squeezing the handle from a safe distance sent a charge of electricity to the mine and *pow!* The mine blew up. These mines could potentially kill two or three, but usually just one person. Claymores were preferred because they were easier to use than hand grenades, and the detonator handle could be squeezed quietly and at a safe distance so as not to give away a US position. Hand grenades were noisy and the thrower usually had to stand up in plain sight to toss the device toward the intended target, thereby giving away his position and exposing himself to enemy fire.

This was Lieutenant's second full day on the ground. The excessive stress, just like the continuous sweat, caused more fatigue than he'd ever thought possible. In the back of his mind was the ever-present thought that the enemy was stalking every American somewhere nearby.

Sullenly, he wondered how many days remained until his rotation back to the States—if he survived. The time spent pre-deployment in California didn't count towards his thirteen – month tour of duty. The count began only after he'd departed the continental limits of the United States two months ago.

Ah, back in the States.

What's my wife doing right now? he wondered. *Sleeping, I'm sure, because there's a thirteen-hour time difference. Is she okay?*

Leaning against a rock, he reached down and unbuttoned the pocket of his uniform trouser just above his left knee to pull out a plastic bag containing his wallet. From inside the wallet he gently lifted a small laminated color snapshot of her smiling back at him. It made him both sad and homesick to see her shining brown eyes. He missed her terribly. His orders had required him to leave home the first week of December 1966, less than six months after they were married.

His mind flashed back to last October on Skyline Drive in the gorgeous Blue Ridge Mountains with a backdrop of scarlet, rust, orange, and golden-yellow trees. It's where he'd taken the picture. Fall was his favorite season, and the weather had been perfect that day: low seventies with a tinge of early morning crispness. The day was just right for a relaxing ride away from the city, through the Virginia countryside and up the lush, winding mountain roads onto the Skyline Parkway that stretched out for miles. They'd spotted a roadside picnic table near a scenic overlook and stopped. She spread out a tablecloth, and they feasted on a leisurely lunch of fried chicken and potato salad that she'd packed early that morning. After lunch, they drove on, enjoying more breathtaking vistas in a glorious array of autumn colors that adorned ridge after ridge of gently rolling mountains. The magnificent scenery greeted the couple at each new turn in the road. Contrasted against a cloudless blue sky, the views were spectacular. With her sitting close beside him, he felt as if he could drive forever. They'd both wished out loud that the day would never end. Both wanted to enjoy nature's colorful, final tribute before winter set in and the time came for his deployment.

He wished with all his heart he could be home with her now.

CHAPTER 2
MISERY AT CHU LAI

FEBRUARY 18, 1967
DAY THREE

Intermittent rain showers fell. Today brought the same drudgery as the day before. They still hadn't reached their destination.
The Lieutenant already despised both the sight and smell of the
red mud that clung to him. It made his clothes starchy stiff despite
the dampness. The blisters on his feet, now open sores, made each
step painful. He knew everyone else's feet felt the same. There was
no point for anyone trying to doctor their feet, because their socks
stayed constantly wet.

Filthy, wet, and hot, the platoon plodded on through their
new hostile environment. They struggled to breathe in the
thick, muggy air. The rice paddies yielded more unwelcomed
insults. When they halted, the Marines took a moment to pick
slimy, black leeches from their arms, legs, chests, and backs under the supervision of the two Navy corpsmen (always called
"Doc") assigned to the platoon. The men used the salt from
their C-ration packets or their government issued talc when
pulling leeches off to keep the slippery bloodsuckers' heads
from breaking away or burrowing further into their skin. The

chemical reaction from the salt or powder caused the parasites to loosen their grip. Leeches only added to the extreme misery the men already felt. The Lieutenant thought he had aged twenty years in two just days.

Along the trek north, the platoon saw where enemy snipers had dug crudely constructed punji pits—concealed holes about four meters deep implanted with razor-sharp bamboo spikes and then disguised with foliage. To fall into one of these, as a few men from the neighboring Third Platoon already had, meant seriously damaging wounds to feet, legs, thighs, or worse.

"Watch where you're stepping," the Lieutenant cautioned his men. "Don't let your guard down. There are land mines and booby traps out there as well."

An unnecessary warning, he knew. All were aware that the Grim Reaper stalked them consistently, just as the seen and unseen insects that attacked them relentlessly. Everyone's nerves were on edge. Nothing was sure. Death was only a cracking sound or an explosion away. Death or dismemberment lurked as nearby as the ever-present enemy. Since early yesterday, platoons in the vicinity had begun reporting mounting casualties. Radio intelligence from the First and Third Platoons had confirmed: one Marine killed; seven wounded. So far, the Weapons Platoon hadn't suffered any killed.

When brief rest periods came, the Lieutenant forced himself to shut down any thoughts of home. He told himself,

I must discipline myself only to dwell on the mission at hand; otherwise, I will lose my edge and my alertness. My life depends on this. I must make this platoon my number one priority—always, he repeated to himself for the thousandth time. *They're depending on me as their leader to make the right decisions.* Yet he still vacillated between wanting to be home and needing to be there attentive, to his men.

FEBRUARY 19, 1967
DAY FOUR

The Weapons Platoon had advanced roughly fifteen miles from the Quan Duc Pho provincial border, south of Chu Lai. With three days behind them and night falling fast, the men of the Weapons Platoon again dug their foxholes like moles burrowing in for the night and attempted to rest.

"Hell, it seems like all we do is dig holes from one end of this stinkin' country to another," the Lieutenant overheard one corporal gripe to his buddy.

Crouched against the side of his foxhole, the Lieutenant again daydreamed about his wife back home, but he was too weary, and the sky had turned too dark for him to write her tonight. The letter home would have to wait. Besides, there was no place to mail it. *She'd be about seven, no maybe seven and a half months along by now,* he mused. The day he'd left, she had gravely looked up at him and solemnly declared, "I hope this baby is a boy so I can name him after you. He'll be a junior. He'll carry your name in case you never get to meet." Now he wondered if he would get to see their child.

He reflected on the bittersweet times they had shared since their wedding day last June. They'd both made a valiant effort to make the best of every moment in the few months they shared together before Vietnam loomed over them. Once again, he chastised himself for obsessing about his wife. But like a persistent habit that can't be overcome, his mind kept drifting back to thoughts of her.

Shortly before midnight, the Lieutenant moved from inside his foxhole and rested beside it on the hard-packed ground. He lay there atop his rubber poncho, trying to escape the intense heat. He was almost asleep, when suddenly an ear-splitting explosion startled him completely awake. A lone enemy soldier had snuck up under the cover of darkness and hurled a hand grenade inside the Marine's perimeter. With that one swift action, rifle rounds flew from all directions, lighting the darkness like frenzied fireflies.

Springing to his feet with the agility of a cat, the Lieutenant pulled the .45 pistol from his side holster and quickly began directing his men as they returned fire. Sometimes crouching low, sometimes duck-walking, but always in constant motion, he moved around the perimeter while yelling encouragements to his troops above the deafening din. This time, his voice was steady.

"Aim low. Keep your rifle and machine-gun fire low, about ten to twenty meters in front of your position. Remember your training. At night you tend to shoot high. We don't want any more of those sons of bitches creeping up on us," the platoon leader cautioned.

"Keep firing!" he shouted again.

It had all happened so quickly, there was only time to react. The Lieutenant's first real encounter with the NVA left him thinking to himself that this was gonna be one long year. He knew the Marines were vulnerable. They had been forced, once again, to react. It showed the Lieutenant firsthand what he long suspected: The US strategy left the offensive to the enemy. Marine training taught men to be the aggressors in war, not just passive defenders.

Counting the grenade tosser, the Lieutenant estimated the attack came from twenty to twenty-five North Vietnamese. The firefight lasted for maybe half an hour. It seemed like an eternity. In the stillness that followed, the heavy smell of gunfire and cordite from the explosions hung in the humid air like a low-slung cloud. For a few seconds, everyone seemed frozen in place. No one moved; not a single person changed position.

For some of the Lieutenant's platoon, the attack was just another encounter. About half the men in Alpha Company had been in combat for varying amounts of time. For others, like the Lieutenant, skirmishes were new. When the platoon had formed in Okinawa in January, some of the men had already served up to six months of their time, while others had just arrived from the States.

A preliminary report from the platoon sergeant confirmed three men lay wounded; everyone else was in one piece. On the field radio, the Lieutenant's superior, Captain R. F. Corcoran, the company commander, immediately called for an emergency medical evacuation (a "medivac") for the wounded men.

Moving hastily around the perimeter, the Lieutenant found Private First Class Soferilla, still conscious, bleeding heavily, and in shock. Part of his right foot was missing; both his boot tip and toes had been blown to bits. Two navy corpsmen assigned to the platoon attended him, and they tied a tourniquet above his ankle to prevent more bleeding.

The Lieutenant stooped down by the stretcher and tried his best to assure the injured man he'd be okay. "An emergency helicopter has been requested, and we're gonna get you out of here and back to the ship in no time. You're gonna be okay." He wasn't sure if Soferilla comprehended.

A few yards away, Private First Class Lauria was down with shell fragment wounds, and Corporal Gowe, lying next to him, was also covered head to toe with shrapnel bits. Both remained alert.

Thankfully, there was no more return fire. An eerie quiet prevailed; the enemy must have fled. Internally, men started processing what had happened. Silently, they began reloading their rifles and checking their weapons and ammo, ever attentive in case the NVA attacked again.

The Lieutenant sat down in his foxhole and leaned his back against the dirt. Carefully, he cupped his hands so as not to reveal any light, and lit a Camel cigarette from his C-rations. By the tiny flame that flickered from his Zippo lighter, he came to the sickening realization that both his hands were covered in blood. Seeing the blood caused adrenalin to pulse through his body. The firefight and its aftermath had claimed all his attention. Instinctively, he began checking his arms, shoulders, and chest to see where the blood was coming from. Finally, touching his face, he felt blood gushing from a gash in his right cheek. That's when he came to the full realization that he, too, had been hit. Surprisingly, he felt no pain.

"Shit," he muttered to no one in particular.

On his feet again, he double-checked to be sure his men had been given all the first aid available and then called out, "Doc, over here!"

The corpsman rushed over, sat him down, and cleaned and taped over the Lieutenant's wound. Next, the corpsman wound white gauze around most of the Lieutenant's head.

As he sat on the ground waiting for the medivac helicopter, the Lieutenant lit another cigarette. He had a thought that would have made him laugh in another place, in another time: *When I inhale, what if the smoke comes out the hole in the side of my face instead of going down to my lungs?*

His own dark humor brought a wary smile to his face. As he took a long, second drag he thought about the irony of how the US surgeon general had recently declared that smoking was hazardous to one's health.

Nothing to do now but wait, he thought. After what seemed like a long time, he heard the unmistakable whirring blades of the rescue chopper coming nearer. Finally, it touched down.

CHAPTER 3
MEDICAL EVACUATION

Private First Class Soferilla, hooked to a blood drip and IV, was loaded aboard the helicopter on a stretcher by the same two corpsmen who'd struggled to stop the bleeding to what remained of Soferilla's foot. Lauria and Gerald Gowe, despite their wounds, managed to walk unaided over to the chopper. So did the Lieutenant. The Lieutenant felt far more concern for his wounded men than he did for himself.

The platoon sergeant, Gunnery (Gunny) Sergeant Middleton, silently assumed command over the platoon. Every man in the platoon automatically understood the chain of command, and no formal words for the transfer of authority were necessary.

The chopper had no seats, so Lauria and Gowe sat on the floor while the corpsmen huddled close to Soferilla. Stretched out prone on his stomach, the Lieutenant hung his head near the helicopter's open side door in an attempt to gulp some fresh air and get some relief from the night heat.

The aircraft lifted enough off the ground to gain sufficient power to fly. Within long seconds, the chopper rose like an awakened beast until it skimmed the treetops, banked, and headed east over a hill for the twenty-minute ride back to the *Iwo Jima* that did double duty as a hospital ship. No enemy fire came up at them.

The Lieutenant knew when they reached water because he saw the sheen of the water's surface in the moonlight. Flying at such a low altitude, he caught sight of the large letters, USS *Iwo Jima* on the stern of the ship. Coming in, the pilot had to pull the aircraft up some distance to land it on the deck. He set the helicopter down as gently as a mother lays a baby in a crib.

Four navy corpsmen were already standing by and ready on the flight deck. Once the chopper landed, with its engine still whining, Soferilla was quickly unloaded and taken to surgery below deck. The others silently followed the directions given by the sailors. The Lieutenant and the two other wounded warriors stepped onto the large open-air elevator. It descended slowly from the flight deck to the hanger deck below where the triage area was located.

FEBRUARY 20, 1967
DAY FIVE

The sterile hospital triage room's stark cleanliness contrasted with the bloody, mud-caked, and grimy appearance of the three walking wounded men. It was late at night, around 1 a.m.

Once in triage, a supply sergeant in spotless, starched utilities met the men with large rubber bags and issued instructions. "Just strip off your gear—helmet, flak jacket, pack, ammo, utility uniform, boots, and weapons. Put everything in these bags. We'll hold it for you in the ship's company storage area."

A corpsman took the Lieutenant's bandages off, and the bleeding from his face resumed. Blood slowly trickled down his face and neck. Naked except for dog tags, the men were ushered into a large shower room along with ten or fifteen other men who had been brought in from nearby platoons. After showering, the Lieutenant was issued a faded blue-and-white striped bathrobe and instructed by a corpsman to lie on a nearby stretcher that rested just inches off the floor in the triage area. Staring at the ceiling above, he waited. At this point, after his adrenaline had slowed, he felt intense pain from the open wound in his face. By then, the bleeding slowed almost to a stop. He wondered how much damage had been done. He speculated that the chunk of an exploded grenade had lodged in the fleshy part of his right jaw. He knew others were being admitted ahead of him because they had worse wounds than he did. The Lieutenant felt bad for those suffering severe trauma.

When he groaned in misery, someone nearby asked, "Have they given you anything for pain yet?"

"No," he managed. Whoever asked must have walked away. He could hear commotion all around him, but lying so low, he couldn't see much. He wondered what would happen next.

SURGERY

After what seemed like an hour or so, a corpsman came by and shot the top of his right thigh full of morphine. The drug had its intended effect. The Lieutenant became groggy, and within seconds, the room began to whirl. He drifted off to sleep, a sleep that did not last long enough. He was awakened by what felt like a stiff wire sticking into his wound. Immediately, the pain intensified. The wire poked around the right side of his face for the shrapnel, and now, regrettably, he was wide awake.

The navy surgeon finally located it, but was unable to extract the large fragment that had penetrated the Lieutenant's cheek and lodged in his jaw area over his molars—so the surgeon just sewed him up. The shrapnel was too close to a nerve that could potentially paralyze the entire side of his face. The Lieutenant vaguely remembered hearing the instruction, "See a plastic surgeon when you return to the States—should you live that long." The Lieutenant floated out of consciousness once again, despite the excruciating pain he experienced.

When he woke up, he found himself bandaged, lying somewhere in the bowels of the ship. He was in the middle of one hundred or more post-op hospital bunks stacked five high with other wounded Marines. The wounded seemed squashed together like crushed cars ready for a junkyard compacting machine. The groaning of so many wounded men in one place sounded like a chorus of doom.

Is this what hell sounds like? the Lieutenant wondered.

When fully awake, his mind and body became aware of the continuous creaking and rocking of the ship. The Lieutenant felt nauseous, and somehow managed to find the head (the toilet). He started throwing up, which made his jaw throb even more.

POST-OP

After a few hours of fitful sleep, he swung out of the makeshift bed and attempted to stand on the floor. With wobbly feet beneath him, he went to check on the others from his platoon. As an amputee, Soferilla had already been airlifted out to a field hospital somewhere in the rear, most likely DaNang. Lauria and Gowe had all the shrapnel picked out of their bodies, and each assured the Lieutenant they would be fit for duty in no time. Both felt they had neither the time nor the inclination for lying around in the ship's hospital doing nothing.

Following the visit to his men, the Lieutenant worked his way up two decks to the ship's vacant lieutenants' rooms without seeing or speaking to anyone. Each tiny room held six hard bunks, a chair, small metal desk, and best of all, was quiet. No one else was around. No one had seen him. No one knew he was there. With his face still smarting and his head heavily swaddled in gauze to keep his jaw stationary, the Lieutenant resembled a cartoon picture of a guy with a toothache. But there was nothing humorous about the way he felt. For the next fifteen hours he lay unnoticed, topside on a bunk in the lieutenant's rooms, still seasick from the constant pitching motion of the ship.

HOW'D I GET HERE?

Unable to sleep, he thought back to the moments in his life that had ultimately brought him to this place. Three years earlier, his draft notice from Uncle Sam had arrived, and he'd enlisted in the Marines. He graduated from boot camp at Parris Island, South Carolina, as top man in his platoon in September 1964. This distinction came with the Leatherneck Outstanding Marine Award, and the accompanying perks included a free dress blue uniform along with his private first class (E-2) stripe. At the time, he felt like he'd been pretty lucky to advance so quickly.

Following boot camp, he spent nearly two boring years guarding nuclear weapons at the Naval Air Station in Jacksonville, Florida, and gained two more promotions to the rank of corporal (E-4). What he really wanted, though, was to be selected for the Navy Enlisted Scientific Education Program (NESEP). If he could gain acceptance to this program, he would be assigned to Bainbridge, the prep school for the Naval Academy. With success at Bainbridge, he would be sent to a university for a degree in engineering. He began studying for the entrance exam in his spare time. Instead, out of the 190,000 enlisted men in the Marines, two hundred, including the Lieutenant, were selected for the Meritorious Non-Commissioned Officer (NCO) Program. In early 1966, he was sent to Officer Candidate School (OCS) at Quantico, Virginia. He would learn to become an officer and a gentleman, a second lieutenant, a "brown bar." He graduated number thirty-three out of the 644 men in his OCS class. Most men in his class held college degrees. Now the Lieutenant had become a "mustang," the Marine moniker for an officer who had at one time been enlisted.

The Marines had no choice but to choose men from the lower ranks for OCS, because it was impossible to keep up with the rate of death among junior officers and senior staff non-commissioned officers (NCOs) who were being killed in Vietnam. The Lieutenant had rightly figured that the Marine big shots needed more cannon fodder for the war, hence his new status. Statistically, the Lieutenant knew his life expectancy in Vietnam was just three months. After the last few days, he knew so now more than ever. He was already a statistic.

I'll probably be dead before the year's up, he thought. *Will I ever get out of this place? Will I go home in a coffin?* He tried to imagine what that would be like, but immediately abandoned the idea as too morbid.

His thoughts once more turned to the wife he left back home.

I wonder if she received the casualty call yet? How'd she react? It must have really scared her. I should get a letter off to her right away. I don't want her to worry. Who knows what she'll be told?

The reality of knowing he had many months remaining on his tour filled him with despair. After less than a week in combat, he was disgusted with both the idea and the reality of war. He felt as if the life he once knew could never be the same. He could only keep going until he got the fatal wound. When it came, he hoped it would come quickly and be relatively painless.

What a schizophrenic existence! I vacillate between thoughts of home and wife and needing to be attentive to the men I lead. Home or combat. Here or there. How do I maintain my sanity?

FEBRUARY 21, 1967
DAY SIX

The Lieutenant decided he had spent enough time convalescing. Pain or not, he knew his duty lay with his men ashore. They were counting on him, and he needed to return to them. He was also tired of constantly throwing up on the rocking ship. He knew his wound amounted to nothing compared to what others had sustained. He knew he couldn't wait for however much red tape it would take to be officially medically released. He'd had enough. He made his choice. He needed to get back to the company storage area, find his gear, get dressed, and catch a resupply helicopter to take him back to Alpha Company in the field. This took less than an hour. He told the supply sergeant, "Give me my gear. I'm headed back to the field." The sergeant complied.

The Lieutenant ditched the blue-and-white robe, donned the dirty, bloodstained uniform and grabbed the rest of his gear. Once up on the flight deck he asked the crew chief, "Which helicopter is going back to Alpha Company, First Battalion? I'm going with it."

The crew chief didn't argue. In fewer than five minutes, he was on his way. Once airborne, the Lieutenant wished the chopper would fly faster. He was ready to get his feet back on solid ground and off the rocking ship. But he was also worried about his absence from his platoon. It was hard to believe his ordeal on the ship had lasted less than forty-eight hours.

When the chopper landed, the Lieutenant walked on shaky legs and reported to his company commander. Corcoran greeted him, surprised.

"Holy shit! What in hell are you doing here?" He shook his head in disbelief.

"Figured I was fit enough for duty, sir."

"Look at you, you son of a bitch!" exclaimed the Captain. "Your helmet barely fits on your head over all those bandages! You look like hell. You're white as a sheet. You should've stayed on the ship. You could have gotten at least three more days rest there."

True, the Lieutenant could have taken a few more days laying in his bunk puking on the *Iwo Jima*. He never imagined his unauthorized absence from the hospital ship would soon cause him to be officially listed as missing in action by the company office on the *Iwo Jima*. He only wanted to be back where the action was.

Word spread quickly about the Lieutenant's adventure secretly slipping away from the ship while still recuperating from his wound. Some of the men from Alpha Company whispered about him with words like, "He's one hard chargin' Marine, ready to do battle."

Every time the Lieutenant protested to the Captain, Battalion Commander, or anyone else that he'd come back to his unit because of seasickness, he was met with, "You're just being modest." It proved to be a futile argument. No one believed him. His reputation became firmly established within the company. The whispering continued for months.

CHAPTER 4

FIGHTING AT CHU LAI AND THE DMZ

LATE FEBRUARY TO MID-MARCH

After nearly a month of search and destroy operations south of Chu Lai, the Weapons Platoon of Alpha Company, First Battalion, Fourth Marine Regiment reversed its initial landing operation. They hoofed it back to a staging area near where the operation had begun. The Marines formed a perimeter south of the original landing zone near where they had first landed in preparation to reboard the USS *Iwo Jima*.

While organizing to re-board the ships, the concentration of so many Marines in one place drew enemy machine gun and rifle fire coming at them from NVA who were hiding in nearby bushes. The enemy waited until the helicopters began landing before they intensified their gunfire. Firing from several directions ensured the enemy's tactic for causing as much confusion as they could. Fortunately, no Marine killed-in-action were reported, although a number of Marines suffered gunshot wounds.

During what should have been a routine troop withdrawal exercise, the situation turned into a major gun battle. The Lieutenant dropped his backpack to return fire. In the confusion of the encounter that ensued, between returning fire and directing the troops, he lost his backpack. What irritated him most was the loss of his small Instamatic camera and several rolls of film that he had taken as mementos of his time in-country. The loss of the backpack paled into insignificance, however, compared to the helicopter pilot who lost his right foot, shot clean off in the firefight. His co-pilot flew the injured pilot back to the USS *Iwo Jima* along with other wounded troops being evacuated. Operation Deckhouse VI: Phase I was now officially over. Phase II was about to begin.

Fourteen hours after re-boarding the *Iwo Jima*, A and B Companies were loaded on twelve helicopters and flown to Sa Huynh, Quang Ngai Provence, a short distance away. The next day, February 26, Phase II of Operation Deckhouse VI began. Alpha Company landed in Sa Huynh amidst heavy rifle and machine gunfire. For the next eight days the Marines engaged in intense fire on a flat scrub brush area near the coast. Their goal was to clear the area of the North Vietnamese Army (NVA) troops.

Fighting continued until March 3. Despite intense gunfire on both sides, the tally from Phases I and II of Operation Deckhouse VI showed Marine casualties were relatively light. The North Vietnamese suffered over 790 NVA killed.

At least we've accomplished something. Despite our losses, we've cleared the enemy out of the area. Hopefully, this will give the civilians some peace. On the other hand, if we don't stay and hold our position, the land might never be secure.

On March 4, the two companies (Alpha and Bravo) left the area and re-boarded the USS *Iwo Jima* with orders to sail east for three days towards the Philippine Islands. Besides the men, shipboard equipment included tanks, artillery, amphibious tractors, (amtracs), and a squadron of helicopters.

The troops were glad to shed their seven-pound flak jackets and heavy helmets. They were able to get hot showers and clean uniforms, and—for those who didn't get seasick—the men could chow down cafeteria style. Of course, the officers dined separately at tables, eating off china plates on linen, but the food was all the same. The Lieutenant ate, but as he expected, he threw it all back up after every meal due to seasickness.

Along with the *Iwo Jima*, three other ships, a full battalion landing team sailed nearby. Corporal Gowe and PFC Lauria, the two wounded Marines who'd been medivaced along with the Lieutenant, rejoined the Lieutenant's platoon before sailing. Others in the company hadn't been so lucky. Sadly, six Marines from Alpha Company had lost their lives and fifty-eight had been wounded during the Chu Lai shootout.

CUBI POINT

The voyage took them to Cubi Point, a small island in the Philippines that was the Special Landing Force (SLF) Camp for admin, resupply, and reorganization. The shipboard trip allowed time for the Lieutenant's platoon to rest and recuperate some.

Upon arrival on solid ground at Cubi Point, officers were billeted in Quonset huts, constructed as half-circular corrugated steel buildings with cement slab floors. The huts were outfitted with cots and each hut housed about twenty officers. There were only a few small, high windows for ventilation. Other Quonset huts were set up as barracks for the troops. They held double bunks, so they housed fifty enlisted men. The mess hall and other administration buildings were also Quonset huts.

At Cubi Point, each man was acutely aware that being in camp was only a temporary respite. They were told ten days, max. In the interim there was always something to keep their minds occupied: get their record books caught up to date and other administrative duties. They could write letters; polish boots; sleep; visit the PX (post exchange) for necessities, etc., but there weren't any regimented activities such as training during this period.

Speculation ran high among the men that their next assignment would be in the Mekong Delta area in southern Vietnam, or possibly at the demilitarized zone (DMZ) in the north. They knew there had been large-scale and intense battles involving battalion and regimental-size American units at the DMZ. Everyone was curious about what their next mission would be. Some hoped the DMZ so they could avoid the swamps of the Mekong Delta region.

MAIL CALL

When they arrived at Cubi on March 8, everyone was pleased to learn that the US mailbag had finally caught up with them. Mail was broken down by company, then further by platoon, and then by squads. So, for example, Alpha Company's mail would arrive in a large mailbag. The company gunnery sergeant would sort the mail into platoons. The platoon sergeant would break it down into squads and then hand it out. All mail from the US to the Lieutenant was addressed in the following manner: rank, name, serial number; A Company, First Battalion, Fourth Marines; Third Marine Division; FPO (Fleet Post Office) San Francisco, California, 96602.

The Lieutenant received a batch of letters from his wife. He and his wife had already learned to number and circle each letter on the return address portion, and also on each page of the letter so when a batch came all at once, they could read each other's letters in sequence. The first one read:

February 21, 1967

My darling,

Last evening while I was fixing dinner, I got a knock at the door. When I went to the door and asked, "Who is it?" the answer was "Warrant Officer Ryan, Headquarters Marine Corps, ma'am." When I heard that, I felt my legs giving out from under me and had to lean against the door and grab the door handle for support. I thought you were dead! When I managed to unlatch the chain and open the door, he looked at my obviously very pregnant self and said right away, "It's not that bad," and that was a huge relief. I had to sit down, though. If I had been thinking clearly, I would have realized that if two men come to the door, and one of them is the Navy chaplain, then that would be it. Anyhow, he was in uniform, and extremely professional, and gave me the very official version, saying something like, "The United States Government regrets to inform you Second Lieutenant . . . was wounded in action on February 19 . . . blah, blah, blah." He gave the barest of details of your wound. He only said you'd sustained a wound to the face, been me-divaced, and that the prognosis is excellent and you would soon return to duty. He also said an official telegram would be coming soon. I thanked him and he left. Despite being formal, he seemed very kind. I called your parents right away to tell them, and I stayed home from work today to wait for the telegram, since it didn't come last night when I expected it. When it finally arrived, it said just about the same as what Warrant Officer Ryan had told me. Still, it was pretty scary, and I'm trying to figure out how badly you are hurt. It's terrible not knowing. Where are you now? How long will you be in the hospital? What happened? Are you really okay? In lots of pain? Will you have a big swashbuckling scar on your face as a souvenir? (Cool!) Please write me back with details as soon as you can. I'm praying you are okay and love you so very much.

All my love

P.S. I thought it was really good the way they sent someone personally to the door to tell me. Pretty classy touch, in my book.

After reading her letter, the Lieutenant thought, *Obviously, our letters have crossed in the mail. I'm surprised she got the wounded notification so quickly. I hope my letter saying I'm okay gets to her soon so she won't worry. I hope she doesn't get another one, or the killed in action one. I wish she didn't have to go through this.*

MARCH 11, 1967
DESTINATION: GIO LINH

It was raining again, a steady, relentless downpour. The Lieutenant sprinted from his quarters to the Quonset hut admin building about fifty meters away. He approached the building at 0655 to hear what the platoon's next assignment would be: DMZ or Mekong Delta, or somewhere else.

Inside the briefing room, metal chairs arranged in rows were set up as straight and perfect as marching Marines. Overhead, a few naked light bulbs hung limply from the ceiling. The Lieutenant chose an aisle chair towards the rear of the room where he could sit for a few minutes by himself in relative silence. He watched the water drip off him into puddles on the cement floor and thought about nothing in particular.

When everyone assembled, those present included the five company commanders; all captains; sixteen lieutenants who were platoon commanders; and the commanders of tanks, artillery, recon (reconnaissance); and shore party. It also included medical officers, the navy chiefs who were senior corpsman, and various other senior NCOs.

At precisely 0700, Lieutenant Colonel "Blackjack" Westerman, battalion commander, stepped in front of the men and began his delivery.

"Our battalion landing team, about 2,500 men strong, will shortly be assigned an offensive landing and operation." Westerman continued, "Operation Beacon Hill will begin in a few days and will last about four months. Our location will be south of the DMZ, about ten miles inland from the South China Sea. Alpha and Bravo Companies will be airlifted by chopper just to the west of the perimeter wire at Gio Linh. Charlie and Delta Companies will land by amphibious tractors and landing craft on the beaches east of Gio Linh and will begin the slow crawl west. Your objective, gentlemen, is to clear the area below the southern border of the DMZ of NVA units and destroy their defensive positions. We'll use bulldozers from Gio Linh to Con Thien, a distance of about seven to ten miles. We will go from east to west and provide security for the Eleventh

Engineer Battalion, who will eventually denude the landscape of trees and other vegetation between those two defensive positions. We want an open space, a trace, about a hundred meters wide and seven miles long. That way any North Vietnamese movement can be easily detected."

Westerman paused for a breath, then continued. "Unfortunately, according to an international agreement, the DMZ is not to be used for military operations, and therefore, theoretically, no one is there. It is a 'no-fire' zone. We all know better, however, so remain on your guard." Another pause. "One last thing: we are forbidden to return fire into the DMZ north of the Ben Hai River. We are only able to defend ourselves between the southern DMZ boarder and the Ben Hai River. Any questions?" Silence. "Gentlemen, that is all."

Holy shit! We'll be sitting ducks! The Lieutenant's heart sank. He realized at once this was a suicide mission. Everyone in the room knew instantly that providing security for the Eleventh Engineer Battalion in an area where they could only return short-distance fire meant every Marine would be in critical danger at every moment. They knew they would be barraged with enemy gun and artillery fire from north of the DMZ.

Well, that's it. It's only a matter of time now. I'll never live through this, he thought. *It's just a fact. Since the summer of 1966, the fighting has been intense in the entire DMZ area.*

Later that night in the officer's quarters, the Lieutenant drank hard and played poker into the early morning hours with three of his fellow lieutenants. They sat shirtless around someone's footlocker, puffing on cheap cigars, making bets, and feigning bravado. Though no one mentioned the upcoming operation, the tension was palpable. It sat like an enormous elephant in the room. The Lieutenant lost all of his spending cash that night, about twenty-five dollars, but didn't much care.

CITATION

The Purple Heart ceremony the following day was a hastily put-together event. Around ten in the morning, eight other recipients along with the Lieutenant, all wearing utility uniforms, lined up outside the admin Quonset hut. The medals were pinned on each Marine in turn by Lieutenant Colonel Westerman.

Hung over, but standing at full attention, the Lieutenant soberly remembered what the surgeon—or someone, he was unsure exactly who—had said about him while he was coming out from under sedation: "He's really lucky! If the shrapnel had hit just an inch higher, it would have gone directly into his brain and killed him; just a bit lower and his jugular would have been severed."

The Lieutenant had difficulty comprehending the enormity of his close brush with death. His jaw still throbbed, even though his head was no longer wrapped in gauze and the entry wound appeared to be healing nicely. Yet the piece of shrapnel still lay entangled somewhere in the muscle and nerve of his jaw.

While waiting his turn to be decorated for wounds received in action, he reflected on those who recently died. *They have not been acknowledged from the time they were medivaced on stretchers or carried off in body bags, nor have they been mentioned here and now. No memorial service, no prayers—nothing. They've just disappeared. Ceased to exist. Those men will never experience this moment, or any other, for that matter. Who gets their Purple Hearts? I guess they send them to their next of kin's address. I'll mail this award home and hope my wife will be glad to have it as a memento when I'm dead. No, on second thought, that would be two Purple Hearts; this one and the one presented posthumously after I'm killed. Families cherish those kinds of things and pass them down through the generations. What a legacy—a hunk of purple medal with a purple ribbon attached.*

The ceremony was over in less than ten minutes. Besides feeling guilty about still being alive, the Lieutenant didn't have time to think too much else about it.

CHAPTER 5

LIFE AT THE DMZ

MARCH 19, 1967
GIO LINH

After a few more days at Cubi Point, the battalion began the methodical process of boarding the USS *Princeton*, a relic ship from the WWII era. The ship had recently been refitted from an aircraft carrier and converted into a more modern helicopter ship. With all the men and equipment ready, they sailed once again for the northeast coast of South Vietnam. The mood was somber as they entered the southern border of the Gulf of Tonkin. The ship came to a standstill about five miles offshore, and parallel to the DMZ, for the start of Operation Beacon Hill.

The Marines disembarked near the coast east of Gio Linh, South Vietnam, and repeated the drill from their first landing. The men of Alpha Company were taken from the ship by helicopter and dropped at their destination about seven miles inland. Both before and after landing, the NVA fired volley after volley of artillery at them from inside the demilitarized zone, technically a "no-fire" zone.

With random artillery fire coming at them, the men wasted no time digging foxholes. There really wasn't any way to take cover.

The terrain was rocky, with some scrub plants and bushes. Together with the few trees, the environment provided little cover. Years before, the area had been used as farmland, but the civilian occupants and land owners had fled long ago, leaving the natural vegetation to take its course.

Hunkered down in two man foxholes out in the open, random booms were heard in the distance and then became screaming projectiles as they came closer. Within three to five seconds after hearing the rumble in the distance, the Lieutenant could identify what was flying towards him and his men: 120mm and 152mm artillery projectiles, about two and a half feet long and ten inches wide; they exploded on impact, shaking the ground beneath the troops. The noise was deafening, and the shrapnel aftermath often ripped through the air at lightening speed. But 122mm rockets or 140mm rockets gave no distant warning. They made a slight swishing sound and a buzz just prior to impact.

Artillery that scored direct hits blew men to smithereens, leaving only bits and pieces of what seconds before were human beings. The explosions propelled upwards chunks of metal, dirt, and flesh. Blood rained back down mixed with the remains of men, dirt, and ordnance.

Loud rumbles reverberated everywhere. Every few minutes, seven to twelve new volleys of artillery fire came in. When they flew nearby, everyone hit the deck. The men had no choice but to dive into their foxholes when they heard but could not see the initial artillery. Its deep rumbling sound rushed at them from across the DMZ. Incoming artillery and rocket fire was interminable, and it continued for days.

When not being fired upon, the troops came out of their foxholes to eat their C-rations and clean their equipment. When necessary, men also came out to relieve themselves. They relieved themselves in record time, because no one wanted to get caught in enemy fire with their trousers down.

Once or twice a day Marines also went on fifteen- to twenty-man patrols, checking to be sure the NVA weren't creeping up on their perimeter defense. Some of these daily patrols or ambush patrols were located up to two hundred meters outside their perimeter. Specifically, these patrols were designed to kill any NVA moving towards the company's perimeter. These patrols could be either partially stationary, or partially roaming, covering every trail, road, or ravine where the enemy could initiate an attack on the Marine's positions.

The Lieutenant ordered, "Go out, set up a spot, and wait for approaching enemy. Open fire once the enemy is in the kill zone."

And that's what they did. When Marines spotted the NVA advancing towards their position, they waited until as many enemy troops as possible had gotten close, then set off Claymore mines and began shooting.

Daily and nightly patrolling often became routine and sometimes tedious. It was easy for the men to slip into complacency and carelessness. The Lieutenant had to constantly remind his men that each patrol was a dangerous mission and could at any time result in a firefight.

When not on patrol, some men tried to read or sleep during the day. Others played cards or checkers. At night, if not assigned to be on alert, the remainder of the men tried to get some sleep. The days were monotonous and nerve-wracking.

Troops received daily food distribution. Several cases of C's were trucked in from the base at Dong Ha. Each platoon received two five-gallon water cans safe for drinking, while each man received two or three boxes containing meals. Work details were assigned to unload the trucks and pass water and food around, effectively serving as an early version of Meals on Wheels.

During the day, about twelve men were pulled off the line to police up the area and collect trash and debris so sanitary conditions would prevail. Another daily task for some of the men was to dig slit trenches, or shit holes, and cover up the old ones. This duty was delegated as punishment to those who had either fallen asleep on duty or incurred some other minor infraction.

The frustration of not being allowed to return fire inside the DMZ reached a high when Second Lieutenant Chuck Lamson, a jolly former gunnery sergeant with eighteen years in the Corps, and a favorite with both officers and men, was hit by shrapnel. He was seriously wounded and medivaced out, barely alive. Word came down from battalion headquarters a short time later that he'd died of his wounds.

In the meantime, between dodging artillery and rocket fire, the job of the Lieutenant's Weapons Platoon was to get their weapons set up and ready as quickly as possible when out on patrol. Weapons included M60 machine guns, the 60mm mortars, and 3.5-inch rocket launchers. They were permitted to fire at any enemy seen on the south side of the DMZ and wanted to be constantly ready. Each platoon member, the Lieutenant included, was required not only to know all the equipment, but how each weapon worked. Every Marine, regardless of rank, had to know how to assemble and disassemble all weaponry.

At Gio Linh, the Lieutenant realized the Vietnam War was not guerilla or insurgent warfare as what he'd seen portrayed in the media before he'd left home.

Perhaps the guerilla warfare was common in other parts of the country, but not at the DMZ. The Marines fighting at the DMZ were engaged in conventional warfare, much like WWII and Korea, with large units engaged in all-out combat with heavy artillery and rockets.

RED CROSS CABLEGRAM

On March 23, while still being fired upon regularly, the Lieutenant and Sergeant Floyd Amos received almost identical Red Cross communications. A private received two radio messages from battalion headquarters from inside the communications center, Gio Linh, about fifty meters away. The private then ran up to the front where the foxhole dwellers were staying. In between artillery salvos, he delivered the two wires, and then hightailed it back to the communication bunker.

The Lieutenant's message read "Congratulations. Your wife gave birth to a boy on March 22. He weighed six pounds, three ounces, and is eighteen inches long. Mother and baby are doing well."

With conflicting emotions, the Lieutenant went from feeling delighted, excited, and proud to intense disappointment for not being at home with his wife. He wished he had cigars to pass out, as he would have back home.

He thought, *Here this little fellow has come into the world who will bear my name, and my wife is all alone—and I'm here. It' just not right. I probably won't ever see either of them. I'll probably never hold my baby son or feel my wife's soft face against mine, but still, I'm so proud to know I have a son and namesake.*

All he could do was yell to whoever was in earshot, "Hey! I'm a dad! My wife just had a boy!"

No cheer went up. No one had heard him above the artillery racket.

A few foxholes away, Sergeant Amos was celebrating the very same event. No one heard his happy shouts either. When comparing their messages a little later, both men were first-time fathers; both babies were born on the same day, and both were boys named

Junior. Regrettably, Sergeant Amos had no cigars to pass out either. Both men's celebrations were limited to a few wild whoops and congratulatory slaps on the back before they dove again into their respective foxholes to take refuge from more incoming artillery. The news of the babies created a stronger bond between the two men.

The Lieutenant felt especially glad to have Sergeant Amos as his platoon section leader. It had been a pleasant surprise a couple of months ago, in early January, when Amos had reported for duty in Okinawa at about the same time as the Lieutenant. It was an even better surprise both men had been assigned to the same platoon. After the mandatory salutes, they shook hands and greeted one another warmly. The Lieutenant and the sergeant had both lived in the same barracks in Jacksonville, Florida. It had only been a little over a year since those days, but it seemed like light years ago. They had gone out drinking together a few times when they were corporals. Both knew and trusted the other.

Floyd Amos possessed an easygoing, pleasant disposition. Additionally, he thrived as a disciplined, conscientious Marine. The Lieutenant respected him and felt Amos was a better man than himself.

Sergeant Amos was thrilled to find the Lieutenant as his new platoon commander, and said so. For his part, Sergeant Amos knew he and the Lieutenant would work well together, but because of protocol, could never be buddies again, as in their earlier days. Both remained respectful of their differences in rank.

CHAPTER 6

LETTER FROM HOME

APRIL 1967

In early April the Lieutenant received a letter from his wife, hand written in her neat penmanship. She described the day the baby was born.

I woke up around five in the morning, and thought I was probably in labor. I waited until the pains were regular, about ten minutes apart, then I called the doctor. My sister drove me to the hospital. Once we arrived, the admissions lady said I couldn't be admitted without my husband to sign me in. She said that's hospital policy for women under twenty-one years of age. I told her you were unavailable.

Well, she looked straight down at my left hand to see if I was wearing a wedding ring. Imagine! I felt like an unwed mother. She wouldn't budge and admit me, so I finally told her in between contractions, "Fine, I'll stay right here and have the baby on your floor."

I'm not exactly sure what happened after that, if they looked up my file to see who my doctor is or what, but guess what? After what seemed like an eternity, but probably more likely fifteen minutes, they finally produced a wheelchair and took me straight up to the labor room. That was about 9 a.m. and our precious son was born at 11:15 that morning. Pretty quick, huh? It wasn't painless, I assure you. Mostly I had back pain, something I hadn't expected.

The baby is adorable, with a head full of dark hair. He's just perfect! He has all his little pink fingers and toes. He is so beautiful! I'll send a picture as soon as I can. The baby might have been bigger if I'd carried him to term, but that's okay. He's doing great, and so am I, so don't worry about us; just take good care of yourself. I miss you awfully, and now even more since we have a baby.

The Lieutenant folded the letter and tucked it into a plastic bag in his trouser-leg pocket, smiling wryly to himself at her tenacity. How he wished he could have been there.

She wouldn't have had to fight that battle with admissions if I'd been there, he thought. All he wanted to do was protect her. Whenever he could spare a few minutes, he reread her letter over and over until the next letters arrived.

MACHINE GUN FIRE

The next day the platoon began their westward attack, evading artillery, rocket fire, and the sporadic hail of bullets that continued to
assault them. The NVA were everywhere; in the DMZ, in the nearby
bushes, lying low in the scrub or in fortified bunkers. Some seemed to
be lone snipers, others were more organized. Sometimes the Marines
were forced to stop for firefights with snipers, and sometimes the
men would walk for several meters without being fired upon. Just before nightfall, they stopped and dug in again. This was their pattern.

Two days later, while digging in a new position, the Lieutenant
was showing the platoon machine gunner, Corporal Greene, where
he wanted him to place his weapon. Just then, the Lieutenant and
Corporal Greene looked up in unison, startled to see an entire
column of NVA, numbering about a hundred men, approaching.
The enemy moved in tactical formation out of the bushes from the
west. The men were small in stature, about five feet five, and most
had scraggly beards. Some wore light-khaki uniforms; others wore
T-shirts and shorts. A few had Vietnamese pith helmets, compara-
ble to US military helmets. Some donned simple cloth headbands.
Apparently, they were moving up to attack Alpha Company's right
flank but hadn't spotted the Lieutenant's platoon.

Instantly, the Leatherneck training kicked in. The corporal
swung the big gun around, and with the Lieutenant feeding the
ammunition belt, they let 'em have it: *Rat-a-tat tat; rat-a-tat tat; rat-
a-tat tat; rat-a-tat tat.*

Once the machine gun fired, the rest of the Lieutenant's platoon realized the danger and opened fire, too. The enemy beat a
hasty retreat back into the bushes, leaving behind three dead NVA
eighty-plus meters away. The incident left the Lieutenant's adrenalin pumping. It was kill or be killed. Still, he felt some remorse for

the dead men. He wasn't so hardened as to deny that the NVA were human beings. He was glad, though, that it wasn't him who was lying dead near the bushes.

That was close, the Lieutenant reflected. *The Death Angel stalks day and night, night and day, just like a hawk seeking its prey. You just don't know when your number will come up.*

FIELD LIVING CONDITIONS

By mid-April the men of the Lieutenant's platoon continued to work their way west. They ate only C-rations; enough to keep them alive, but barely enough to keep their hunger at bay. The Lieutenant's wife regularly mailed him hot sauce to kill the taste of his C-rations. He carried it in his pack and put it on everything he ate. It was common knowledge that hot sauce would prevent intestinal issues; consequently, the Lieutenant never developed dysentery or became infected with parasites. If a man did get dysentery and it was a one-time occurrence, the corpsman would distribute medicine to him. If the dysentery persisted, the man would be medivaced for further treatment.

While subsisting in the field, the men shaved using their helmets to hold water from their canteens, yet without the added luxury of shaving cream. Occasionally they brushed their teeth. Men were issued one very small tube of toothpaste that they rationed to themselves. They wanted the toothpaste to last as long as possible, and only used it when their teeth became so mildew-like fuzzy that they were obliged to scrub. Toilet paper was a coveted commodity. It came in small tan-colored sheet packets wrapped in brown paper. It was imperative to keep this "treasure" dry inside their backpacks, because once wet, fingers could easily poke through the paper during use, an experience everyone wished to avoid.

RATS

After ten days, the men of Alpha Company were ordered to retrace their steps back to Gio Linh's perimeter. No explanation was given for the order. Once A Company returned to Gio Linh, their mission was to take up the perimeter defense. The perimeter area around the Gio Linh defensive positions had bunkers, hastily built sometime before their arrival. They were made from old ammo boxes filled with dirt and sandbags. The bunkers only reached about four feet high on the inside, so it was impossible to stand up. Nevertheless, they were considered by some to be slightly safer and a little more uptown than foxholes. But the Lieutenant despised living in bunkers more than in foxholes. At least from the foxhole he could see the horizon, something impossible from inside a bunker.

The bunkers were putrid smelling. They reeked from body odor. With eight men packed inside and only a few tiny portholes for ventilation, the Lieutenant ardently hoped nobody inside farted. Small candles burned continually to add light, making the bunkers even stuffier. Combined with the intense heat and lack of fresh air, it was impossible to sleep for any period of time while inside a bunker.

At night the constant sound of rats scratching on the wood artillery ammo boxes inside the bunkers meant another nerve-wracking distraction. A bunker would contain six makeshift bunks, about two feet off the ground, made out of wooden planks. These planks were nailed together and set on top of stacked, empty ammo boxes.

One night, during an artillery attack lull, the Lieutenant stretched out on his back on a hard bunk and nodded off. When he awoke, a pair of eyes were staring him in the face. It took him a few seconds to realize the eyes belonged to a big black rat, the size of a cat. The creature stood on the Lieutenant's chest as if contemplating him. The Lieutenant swiped it away hard with one hand

45

and jumped up, bellowing, "Get the hell off me, you dirty bastard!" sending the rodent scurrying off into the night. The Lieutenant found the incident creepy. Big, nasty vermin were just a fact of life at Gio Linh.

COMPANY REORGANIZATION

During the time at Gio Linh, Captain Corcoran decided to reorganize the members of each platoon in his company due to the high number of causalities and the lack of live bodies to replace them. He also reassigned each platoon commander. The Captain thought it was equally important to increase every platoon commander's alertness by reassigning them. He didn't want his officers to become complacent in their relationship with the men under their command. So the Lieutenant was changed from Weapons Platoon commander to Second Infantry Platoon commander. Every lieutenant in the company, plus the executive officer, was reassigned new duties with different platoons after being together for the past four months. The troops didn't like the decision. They grumbled out loud about the change. The men had developed loyalties and attachments to their individual platoon commanders.

The Lieutenant, reassigned from the Weapons Platoon, to the Second Platoon, was well received there. He knew many men in the Second Platoon already. The Marines from both the 3.5-inch rocket launcher section and 60mm mortar sections were reassigned as riflemen in other A Company platoons. This was done for two reasons: First, both weapons were deemed ineffective against the NVA; the deadly back-blast from the 3.5-inch rockets often injured those firing them. The 60mm mortar did not have an effective range for reaching the enemy. It was no match for the NVA's 82mm mortar.

Second, both weapons were too bulky and heavy to carry. In truth, they were antiquated. The machine gun section of the Weapons Platoon was divided equally among the three rifle platoons with two machine guns each. The Weapons Platoon now only existed on paper.

M16 DEBACLE

It was while living in foxholes and bunkers at Gio Linh that the order came down from on high, specifically from General William C. Westmoreland himself. Westmoreland, the US Army Commander in Chief of all forces in South East Asia, ordered all M14 rifles be replaced by the newer M16 rifles. So right there in the field, in foxholes, on patrols, and in the rear, both army and Marine troops, and anyone else who carried an American-made rifle, were relieved of their weapons and handed M16 rifles en masse.

Leathernecks pride themselves on being able to completely disassemble and reassemble their weapons blindfolded while simultaneously naming all the parts—a routine part of their basic training. Not only did the servicemen in-country receive no training in the new weapons, they also found out that the damn things jammed when firing, causing many deaths. It quickly became obvious to everyone that the M16 was an inferior weapon to the older M14.

The new rifles continually malfunctioned, and the men felt as if they had become like ducks in a shooting gallery, ready to be picked off for sport. Obviously, the M16s and the gunpowder in the M16 bullets had not been properly tested before being distributed to those in combat. The entire military population was riled up over the situation, from the big brass right down to the young man in the foxhole. They complained about it for months, and resentment ran high. Some smart private came up with the expression "The M16 is swell. It's made by Mattel" (referring to the popular US toy manufacturer's motto).

It was later discovered that the gunpowder for the bullets was inferior. The bullets were hurriedly mass-produced and didn't match the specifications for the weapons. The powder was entirely the wrong chemical composition and caused the rifles to misfire or sometimes just jam.

Out in the open area around Gio Linh one day while on patrol, the Lieutenant test-fired one of the new rifles. His frustration boiled over. He threw the M16 on the ground in anger, exclaiming, "How the hell are our men supposed to fight with this piece of shit? This is blatant incompetence. Complete bullshit. Probably there's some fat, sleazy politician in Washington, sitting on his big ass, getting a nice kickback on this junk at the expense of us poor suckers stuck here in combat! Don't they realize men are dying because of this?"

Then he let loose with a stream of profanity. The men in his platoon completely agreed and readily voiced their opinions to the Lieutenant with similar enthusiasm.

The new rifle reminded the Lieutenant of his early days in-country. When he first disembarked from the *Iwo Jima* in mid-February, he had lugged around an old Thompson sub-machine gun, given him by a fellow platoon commander. He carried it on his shoulder in a sling, fixed so the weapon always pointed outwards. It fired two rounds before jamming, every time. The Thompson sub-machine gun was a holdover from the days of Prohibition and was more for show than for real. As long as he carried it, the Lieutenant felt it made him look "bad," like a gangster. After about a week, he tired of it and gave it away to a sergeant who was delighted to receive the gift. The M16, by comparison, was serious business, and lives depended on the weapon to function properly, which it clearly did not.

THE TRACE

After occupying Gio Linh for a week, Company A initiated a full-
fledged attack on nearby NVA to clear the area from Gio Linh all
the way to Con Thien, a distance of about ten miles. The width
of the trace measured about a hundred meters wide. The mission
for Alpha Company, per their battalion commander, Lieutenant
Colonel Westerman, was to provide security for the engineers.
The engineers would begin stripping the foliage on this narrow
piece of land from Gio Linh west to Con Thien. This strip became
known as "the trace." The trace security mission was unpleasant.
The men were constantly on the move and out in the open around
heavy equipment that made tremendous noise. The only way the
men knew they were taking enemy fire was when they saw the explosions or saw their buddies fall from gunfire. They couldn't hear
even small arms or machine gunfire.

AMBUSH

The next morning, still heading toward Con Thien while providing security for the bulldozers, the First and Second Platoons
suddenly started taking fire. Everyone dropped to their stomachs
to return the barrage. Besides artillery, they were taking fire from
82mm mortars. When the ambush was over, the man laying to the
Lieutenant's right didn't get up. He remained where he dropped as
if frozen in place.

So the Lieutenant called out, "Hey, you okay?"

No answer. The man didn't move. The Lieutenant checked his
pulse, stunned to find him dead. Of course, he'd seen men die already, but this Marine had been less than five meters away. When

the Lieutenant turned him over, he could see the man had sustained wounds to his entire body with multiple shrapnel bits from an 82mm mortar. He knew the man had been hit by an 82mm mortar by the sound it had made: *thump, thump, thump, swish.* Definitely it had been a mortar that had gotten him. The Lieutenant knew that it could have just as easily been him lying there. The man was from the First Platoon, and the Lieutenant didn't know him. The Grim Reaper's reach had come a little too close.

The Lieutenant felt sadness for the man and anger toward the enemy for taking the life of the young fighter. *War's just not fair*, the Lieutenant thought. Still, seeing men die every day, all around, filled the Lieutenant with rage and sorrow. The Lieutenant, as their leader, knew he had to turn his own emotions inward so his men wouldn't become demoralized by the constant loss of life all around them.

The Lieutenant checked the man's ID. He found the man's wallet stuffed in a plastic bag in his pocket. Inside was a picture of a smiling young woman, presumably the man's wife or girlfriend.

How will she react when she gets the news that he is dead? he wondered. *Another good man going home early—in a wooden box. Damn.*

The Lieutenant knew the fight wasn't over. There wasn't even time to mourn. Instead, he called for a corpsman to come and tag the dead man. The corpsman wrapped the private up in a poncho because all the body bags had been used. Ponchos used in place of body bags were standard procedure when all body bags had been exhausted.

The newly deceased, along with the few wounded, were gently loaded onto a medivac helicopter, then flown to Dong Ha to a field hospital.

The Lieutenant hated seeing men get killed. He hated hearing them scream out in excruciating pain when they got hit. He hated that there was little he could do to help them. He hated this damn godforsaken country and the stupidity of how this random, futile war was being conducted. He knew it was starting to take its toll. Mentally, he flipped the bird at the Grim Reaper.

Okay. In the end, you'll win, he declared defiantly to himself. *I'm a dead man, but I'm gonna taunt the hell out of you before it's all over.*

THE BIG GAMBLE

This is what he did: When the Lieutenant heard the sound of incoming, he deliberately waited until he knew it was the very last possible second before impact, then he took cover. Other men played this game too—seeing how long they could cheat their untimely demise. It became a sick joke. Listen for incoming, identify the type of ordnance; *wait, wait, wait, now! Dive for the foxhole!* The Lieutenant no longer felt fear or apprehension. The game broke the monotony of seeming impending death. Playing was an all-or-nothing gamble, and some lost.

PLACING THE TOWER

At the end of April, another order came for the Lieutenant's platoon to go back, once again, to the area west of Gio Linh. This time, their mission was to provide additional security for a detachment of the Eleventh Engineer Battalion. The engineers would prepare an area for a tower that would be helicoptered into position. The remainder of the company—the other three platoons of Alpha Company—continued their attack to the west in order to reach Con Thien.

The tower was to be the first of about seven or eight spy towers placed at the DMZ. The engineers had to drill large holes in which to ground the first tower. The tower would then be equipped with night observation devices and cameras so US forces could observe the NVA when the enemy attempted to cross the cleared strip.

That night, after the engineers had finished digging the holes, Gio Linh was barraged with all manner of incoming. From north of the DMZ came artillery rounds, rockets, and mortar fire. The Marine artillery at Gio Linh fired back into the southern sector below the Ben Hai River because it was forbidden by international truce for the Marines to fire north of the Ben Hai River, which was part of North Vietnam. The battle was fierce. More than three thousand rounds of NVA artillery exploded at Gio Linh during the night in the faces of the Marines. The artillery exchange was so intense that all the tires on the big US artillery guns went flat. Shrapnel had torn the tires apart. The Marines' supply of ammunition was dangerously low. They dreaded running out and nearly did.

During the fighting, the Lieutenant and his platoon were situated by the tower holes out in the open, about a mile west of Gio Linh. As dusk approached, they could see the NVA units crossing the DMZ and heading east toward the Gio Linh perimeter. Some of the enemy wore olive-drab (green) uniforms. Others wore a variety of uniforms. One guy was wearing a white shirt.

The Lieutenant, manning the field radio, monitored two separate conversations using two different frequencies. The first one was with the Alpha Company commander near Con Thien, where the Second Platoon had left the company. The other conversation was conducted with the US Marine artillery battalion commander at Gio Linh. Initially, the Lieutenant reported in to his company commander the following: "NVA troops moving in towards the east from the west. Looks like a battalion or more. They just spotted us! They've held up! It looks like they're ready to launch a ground attack against Gio Linh!"

He also reported the same to the artillery battalion commander located in a command bunker at Gio Linh.

Just then, the enemy's big guns began reverberating in the distance. They streamed towards the Second Platoon's position out by the tower holes. The Lieutenant could see their aim was way off. They were overshooting about a hundred meters or so behind his perimeter, sailing far over everyone's head. However, the Lieutenant chose not to say anything into the field radio, because he knew the enemy was monitoring all communications. So he maintained radio silence regarding his position, not wanting to give away his platoon's exact location.

At the same time, about four miles southeast, a convoy of about twenty or twenty-five trucks had been dispatched from the south along Route 1 from Dong Ha. The trucks carried ammo, reinforcements, and equipment. They made it almost to the Gio Linh perimeter, about three miles away, when NVA ground forces with small bazookas attacked the convoy. An enormous explosion occurred. Every truck was hit. The explosion blast noise and resulting fireball could be seen and heard for miles. The Lieutenant's platoon could only surmise what was happening, as they were not in the thick of the battle. The firing went on all night. By dawn, things gradually quieted down.

Over the radio, the Lieutenant heard Lieutenant Colonel Bill Rice, of the artillery battalion ask incredulously, "We've taken all these rounds and we are not allowed to shoot back?"

The Lieutenant thought the lieutenant colonel must have been a recent replacement. He seemed to be unaware of the rule about firing north of the Ben Hai River above the DMZ.

Someone else replied into the radio, "It's a no-fire zone."

"Well, let me tell you what your no-fire zone has done to our men!" Rice angrily replied in complete exasperation.

The Lieutenant wondered if the lieutenant colonel was addressing his own superior officer.

MCNAMARA'S FOLLY

During the time of clearing the trace from Gio Linh to Con Thien, all the while providing the security to cover the tower installation, the Lieutenant, as well as everyone else, realized the stupidity of installing the towers. After seeing the first tower installed, they recognized that placing a whole line of towers was a complete waste of time, reminiscent of the Maginot Line.

After WWI, a series of bunkers (concrete fortifications in a row or line) were built on the eastern border between France and Germany to keep the Germans from attacking France. Later in WWII, the Germans simply went around to the northwest to attack France through the Ardennes Forest.

Similarly, instead of coming south through the DMZ, the enemy could just come around from the west through Laos. The towers would be totally useless in spying on the enemy. It was basic logic for the NVA: If you can't go through, then go around. The Lieutenant groaned inwardly thinking about the many lives that would be lost while putting the towers in place. He was amazed that such ignorance existed in the Washington-generated strategy.

Everyone seemed to understand the futility of the tower placement except the bespectacled, intellectual Secretary of Defense, Robert S. McNamara. Apparently, the whole foolhardy plan was his idea. He possessed plenty of brains, but it seemed to the Lieutenant the Secretary of Defense had no idea of the practical. The men reserved their choicest words for McNamara. Any derogatory expletive imaginable didn't quite capture just about every Marine's feelings for the politician who didn't seem to know his ass from first base.

The next day, with the first tower installed, the men of the Lieutenant's platoon started moving in formation west for Con Thien to rejoin Alpha Company. Bravo Company had replaced them at the tower. Once again, the Second Platoon continued the westward attack. Along the way there were a few skirmishes, but no casualties. They worked their way west for a full day until unexpected orders arrived. Three hours later, helicopters swooped down and ferried the entire Second Platoon to Dong Ha for a few days rest.

Within a month, the NVA blew up the tower the engineers had installed. Then the NVA skirted around the DMZ to the west and came south through Laos, as predicted.

SHORT BREAK

The men were grateful for a break. They were given five days to clean their (inadequate) new rifles, rest up, and write letters home. For a few, it would be their last communication. The two best aspects about being in the rear were taking a shower from a rigged up fifty-five-gallon drum barrel and eating hot chow from the mess tent. Even though the food was tasteless, it surpassed C-rations.

At Dong Ha, the Lieutenant received a fresh batch of letters from his wife. She wrote almost daily. It was rare for him to receive mail from anyone else. Occasionally, his mother wrote, too. She didn't have much to say except for urging him to remain alert. She wrote as if she had an insider's view of war. She had been born at the Marine Corps Recruit Depot at Parris Island, South Carolina, the daughter of a WWI warrant officer. Her father, the Lieutenant's grandfather, was a stern man. He'd fought in France at both Belleau Wood and Chateau Thierry, and had the stories and medals to prove it. His war stories generally came out after he'd had a few stiff drinks, which happened quite often.

For some reason, the Lieutenant's dad never wrote. His father had served as a Marine in both WWII and Korea. Due to his poor eyesight, though, he'd spent his war years either at Headquarters Marine Corps or Camp Lejeune, North Carolina, at desk jobs. He never left the States to fight. He was a quiet, kind man, and the Lieutenant knew his dad loved him. The Lieutenant didn't understand why his dad didn't write; however, his mother's letters seemed to speak for both his parents.

The Lieutenant's wife's letters, on the other hand, were much more interesting. He arranged her letters in sequential order and read them one by one until he'd almost memorized every line. His wife had begun taking snapshots of the baby. Sometimes her sister took the picture, so a photo might show his wife with his son. When the film was developed, she'd enclose one picture with each letter. He welcomed those pictures, along with detailed descriptions of the baby's latest developments. One picture, which the Lieutenant placed inside his helmet, showed the infant in a tub of water. His wife was laughing and holding the baby up. The chubby boy wore a huge grin on his toothless face, like he was laughing at the idea of a bath.

The best part of those letters was when his wife assured him of her undying love. She often confessed how desperately she missed him. Though her words made his heart sing, he also felt overwhelmingly homesick and longed to see them both as he read the letters again and again.

Sometimes he didn't know what to think. He vacillated between knowing he'd be killed and hoping against hope that he really would make it home alive. At night his dreams were about his wife.

What would it be like for her to be widow? How would our son grow up without his father? No, I won't think about that now.

Drifting off to sleep, he recounted her tender words to him from her letters.

CHAPTER 7

ON TO CON THIEN

EARLY MAY 1967

Being in Dong Ha for a few days, removed from the close combat at the DMZ, boosted the platoon's morale. Physically, the men were somewhat rejuvenated, too. At least their bellies were full, their hair cut, and their bodies clean. A few replacements had joined the platoon, but consistently, the number of new men who joined grew less than the number of those who had been lost.

We'll never win anything at this rate. The pattern is lose ten men, replace with seven, the Lieutenant silently fumed.

"Lieutenant, I've got some good news for you," the company commander said just before Alpha Company headed out again, this time for Con Thien. "The order has finally come down that we can return fire into or across the DMZ. At long last we are permitted to fully defend our positions."

"It's about time those SOBs in Washington got their asses in gear," the Lieutenant replied wryly. "The powers that be have finally seen the light."

But why has it taken so long? Don't they know men are dying here every day because the NVA never respected the international agreement?

Before they left the relative safety of Dong Ha, the Lieutenant told his platoon, "We're going by chopper to Con Thien to rejoin the company."

He didn't need to explain further. Every man knew Con Thien's location. It sat on a hill, a gradual incline, just north of them. Each man knew the danger. Con Thien was situated like a huge zit on the face of the flat, scrub brush earth at the DMZ. It was almost constantly under attack. Since the year before, more men had been killed or wounded on that one hilly area than in all other Vietnam battles along the DMZ.

"Con Thien's a very vulnerable position. Intense fighting. They've had so many casualties there," the Lieutenant commented almost absently to Staff Sergeant Collins, his platoon sergeant.

"Yes, sir," came the terse reply and serious look.

There was nothing else to say. Both men had seen the casualty reports. Both had a fair idea of what they were in for.

That day, two CH-46 helicopters, each carrying about fourteen men, made two round trips to get the platoon to Con Thien's landing zone. Rather than using a low-level approach to the south side of the hill, the choppers came in high at an altitude of two thousand feet, giving the enemy a perfect chance to shoot at them. The Lieutenant didn't understand why.

Maybe they're new pilots and just don't know the danger, he conjectured.

From that altitude, the aircraft began spiraling down for the landing. This landing method served as a general announcement to all North Vietnamese that the replacements were coming in—and meant the enemy could re-load and begin shooting at them anew. But for some reason they didn't.

Captain Corcoran had arrived by foot with the three other platoons from his company a few days earlier. Now he stood at the edge of the landing zone pointing the way for the Lieutenant and the Second Platoon to run from the choppers to the south side of the hill. They ran because no one could be sure when the gunfire would begin again, and with the noise from the helicopter, gunfire could not be heard. From the landing zone, the Lieutenant commanded the men to take up their defensive positions in foxholes. The previous company that had occupied the hill had already dug these out. Con Thien had a few badly constructed bunkers near the north side of its surface, but nobody thought they were any safer than the foxholes.

Platoon-size patrols began around the area and lasted for about twelve hours during the daylight. At night, in front of each squad there was a two-man listening post. About fifty meters further out, there was a squad of fifteen men with a machine gunner. These men acted as another listening and observation post. On clear nights while listening, they also strained their eyes by moonlight to see if they could notice any movement coming towards them. The purpose of the outposts was to provide early warning of approaching enemy troops and to initiate gunfire against anyone seen moving towards the hill. The patrols remained constantly on the lookout for NVA. In addition to the listening posts, each company (Alpha and Delta) would send out an ambush patrol about five hundred meters away from the perimeter. The intention was to open fire on any approaching enemy forces and to provide additional security for the perimeter.

OLD MAN AND A BABY

One bizarre daytime incident happened around May 5 or 6. On a small hill, just outside the perimeter to the southwest of Con Thien, a Second Platoon corpsmen heard what he thought sounded like a baby crying. There had been no Marine awareness of any civilian population living in the immediate area since 1966. As the doc drew closer to inspect, he found an abandoned straw hut. Inside there was an old man, dead on the floor. Lying nearby was an infant girl who looked to be about two months old. The baby was bundled up in rags, and wailing. The doc radioed the Lieutenant, who requested a medivac. The corpsman tagged them both and put them on an outbound helicopter. The baby would most likely be placed in an orphanage somewhere. The Lieutenant didn't know what would be done with the old man's remains.

Together, the Lieutenant and the corpsman reasoned it was likely the old man, maybe the grandfather, was carrying the baby while trying to get someplace safe, away from the NVA. He wasn't bloated, so he couldn't have been dead for long, but his cause of death was a mystery. They surmised that he must have recently come out from the mountains just to the west.

DUTY AT CON THIEN

Terrain at Con Thien was scrubby with hedgerows, just like the terrain to the east at Gio Linh. Enemy artillery and rocket rounds went off regularly, about every five to ten minutes. No one slept. But occasionally the men could catch an hour or two of sleep curled up in fetal position in their dirt foxholes.

While on patrol, there was no place to take cover. All the men could do was drop flat on the ground when they heard incoming and hope for the best. The Lieutenant stayed in touch with the company commander by radio.

"This is Alpha Two," the Lieutenant called in using his radio identity.

"Alpha Six here," Captain Corcoran replied.

"All men in position, sir. We're at 50 percent alert [half resting, half watching, and listening at the ready with weapons in hand]. We'll set the radio watch as per usual."

"Roger that," Corcoran said.

In addition, each platoon kept their radios on all night. One radio was held by the squad leader at the outpost, and one radio, in the defensive position was controlled by the Lieutenant. Radio watch, as it was called, was divided into three-hour increments. The Lieutenant, the platoon sergeant, and the platoon guide by turns kept in constant contact with the squad outside the perimeter. The company commander stayed in contact with the Lieutenant, but used a different frequency.

"Alpha Two, this is Fox," came the check-in call from the squad leader outside the perimeter. His was a familiar voice, so there was no question that it was the squad leader, Corporal Alvarez, speaking.

"Fox, this is Two," came the Lieutenant's reply.

"All positions secure."

"Okay."

This was the nightly routine. Each night different squads rotated, so duty came up every three nights. Delta Company had an identical ambush squad to Alpha Company's. In addition to the ambush squad, each platoon manned a listening post about thirty or forty feet in front of the perimeter.

The nightly routine was about to take a deadly turn.

CHAPTER 8

THE BATTLE OF CON THIEN

MAY 8, 1967

Roughly 450 Marines occupied Con Thien Hill with Alpha Company, located on the south side, and Delta Company on the north side. The helicopter landing zone took up the middle, flat part of the hill.

On the evening of May 7, the Lieutenant sent out the second squad of his platoon for ambush watch, led by Corporal Enrique Alvarez. His squad was in a location to the northeast of Delta Company's position on Con Thien Hill. Delta Company was on the north side of the hill. The Lieutenant tried to maintain radio contact with the squad during the night, but the enemy sometimes jammed the radios, making contact spotty, at best. On that night, all radios were jammed.

At precisely 2:55 a.m., May 8, all hell broke loose. First, artillery boomed in the distance, radiating a green glow in the sky. Incoming landed on the Delta Company side of the perimeter just seconds later. Rockets followed, hitting directly on Company D 's bunkers and defense positions. Fire, dirt, shrapnel chunks, and pieces of wooden ammo boxes burst in the air into enormous blasts. In a matter of just a few minutes, roughly three hundred rounds of artillery had savagely attacked the Marines' position.

Realizing a large-scale battle had begun, about ten men from both Alpha Company and Delta Company who were manning the looking and listening posts outside the perimeter, scrambled back to their defensive positions. Corporal Alvarez and his squad were too far outside the perimeter to safely return, so they remained in place.

While NVA artillery was shelling the hill, the enemy started bringing up their sapper units. These units were made up of about fifty boys as young as around ten or eleven years old. Sappers' made up a demolition team because of the explosives that were strapped to their bodies. They were instructed to lie down across the barbed wire and then ignite the explosives. These boys were used to destroy the barbed wire around the perimeter in order to open a path for the attacking force. The kids were slaves, captured in villages in the north by the NVA and forced into service. All sappers eventually died in explosions. Death was their ultimate mission. Using children as live weapons was one of the most despicable and inhumane tactics the NVA employed.

The sappers' explosives tactics worked. Some time around four in the morning, the North Vietnamese managed to infiltrate D Company's position. They broke through the barbed wire and penetrated Delta Company's side of the perimeter.

In an all out attack, the enemy began climbing the hill; probably two regiments of them, numbering about three thousand men. The Marines, less than five hundred strong, fired back, but their M16s kept jamming. The scene was utterly chaotic. Men fell and died all along the perimeter. Some screamed as they were hit, some fell silently. Casualties mounted steadily.

When the attacking forces started up Con Thien Hill, it was impossible to tell from which direction the main force was coming. It was probable that the enemy sent out a few men to create a diversion while the remaining enemy troops came from a different direction. Coming from the southwest made the most sense, because they had the mountains to cover their approach to Con Thien hill.

Rifle rounds and gunfire bursts splintered everywhere. The night flashed like daylight. The enemy had managed to jam the US radios so communication among the US units was only minimally possible. The Lieutenant couldn't advise anyone else of what was going on at his location. He couldn't radio in artillery or air support. No American on Con Thien could call in anything: not the other platoon commanders, the company commander, or the battalion executive officer. The cacophony of sound overpowered any chance for voice commands to be heard by the men except at the squad or fire team level. Rockets swished close by, then exploded in flashes of white and loud booms. Showers of flames, smoke, and shrapnel pelted down all around. Delta Company fought hand to hand with the North Vietnamese for hours.

God, please help us. Show me what to do, the Lieutenant silently pleaded with the Almighty. Even if he'd called out his prayer, it would not have been heard above the noise of the battle.

Heavy artillery persistently thundered from the distance. Whistling and whooshing, unrelenting explosives seemed to stream from everywhere. The sound rumbled, echoed, then screamed in the night before crashing close by, leaving fiery pits burning all around. It seemed like hell itself had opened up.

The *rat-a-tat* of heavy machine gunfire continued unabated. Rifle cracks sounded everywhere, including the distinctive sound of the enemy's AK-47 assault rifles. Thuds and reverberations shook the ground. In ferocious fighting, the earsplitting noise became deafening, and only grew more intense as the minutes passed.

As ordered, Company A remained on complete alert, watching and waiting for their chance to attack the advancing NVA. The men from A Company knew that D Company was being attacked ferociously, yet Alpha Company had orders to remain stationary. Gunfire rounds and blinding bright explosions continued to blaze in the night sky. The light from the blasts seemed like lightning strikes. Bedlam reigned. All manner of incoming rounds flew directly at, near, over, or around the fighters.

Seventy meters away from D Company, on the other side of the perimeter, the Lieutenant paced the defensive line.

Walking back and forth, he instructed his men, "Hold your position until we know which direction the main force of the enemy is coming from. Keep your eyes open. I repeat, riflemen: remember to aim low towards the ground. It looks like we're gonna be in for one hell of a long battle. Stay in touch with the man on your left and the man on your right. Weapons section: make sure your machine guns are loaded and ready to fire. Get all your ammo ready. Steady now."

The Lieutenant's main intent was to demonstrate that he was present with his men, and not cowering in a foxhole. He wanted his men alert, calm, and focused. Alpha Company faced south. By now, everyone knew the attack had come from the north. The men from Alpha Company also knew with certainty they'd be the next ones to run across the landing zone to reinforce Delta Company's position. They waited in tense expectation for the command.

"Load up with extra bandoliers of ammunition for the attack! We don't want to run out, and we can't be resupplied!" the Lieutenant shouted to his squad leaders.

Nearly an hour had passed, with the action still going full fury. Major Boyd, the battalion executive officer, and Captain Corcoran shared the same bunker on Con Thien Hill. Major Boyd then instructed Captain Corcoran to reinforce Delta Company using Alpha Company because Delta was running out of ammo and could no longer hold their defensive line.

The radios continued jamming intermittently, but the Captain finally got through to the Lieutenant.

"I'm taking two squads from Alpha's First and Third Platoons to reinforce Delta Company!" Corcoran yelled into the radio. Then he continued, "Second Platoon, you will be on standby to back them up."

The Lieutenant repeated the Captain's plan of action to his men in the Second Platoon, adding, "Now we're gonna punish those bastards for attacking us! Start loading up your weapons and equipment!"

Corcoran took a squad from the First and Third Platoons of Company A, about twenty men. He also took two sections of machine guns, about eight men, and directed them into two armored amtracs. The plan was to drive the amtracs over to Delta Company on the north side, to reinforce Delta's perimeter and bring resupplies of ammo. They were quickly loaded and on the move. However, the first amtrac that attempted to cross the open space (helicopter landing zone) got caught in the barbed wire around the perimeter and couldn't move. That blocked the second amtrac, leaving both amtracs immobile and vulnerable. Then both amtracs took direct hits from RPG rockets. The ammo inside the amtracs instantly exploded. The men inside became engulfed in an inferno. The trapped men tried to drop the ramp on the front of the amtracs so they could escape. Only a few made it out safely. Mortars alongside the artillery continued to shower both A and D Companies. The air streamed with bullets and machine gun rounds that continued to pelt like a sideways rainsquall. Corcoran, on the radio, ordered the Lieutenant to move from the Second Platoon's defensive positions

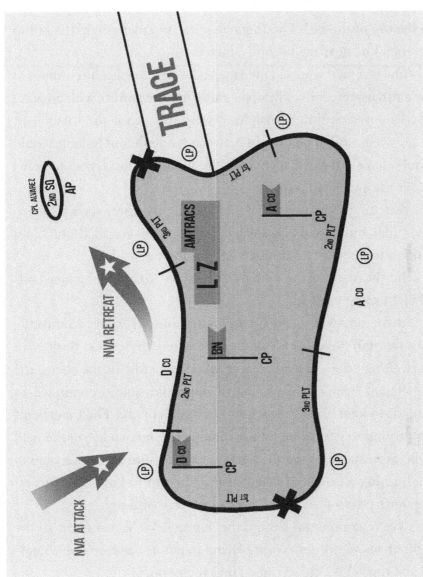

BATTLE OF CON THIEN

LZ: Landing Zone

CP: Command Posts

NVA: North Vietnamese Army

PLT: Platoon

BN Battalion

LP: Listing Posts

AP: Ambush Patrol

SQ: Squad

CO Company

to the top of the hill. The Lieutenant led the platoon up the hill to a trench line near the burning amtracs.

The few men who had managed to escape the deadly confines of the amtracs were left in the open under intense gunfire with no place to take cover. Still not daylight, it was difficult for the Lieutenant to see what was happening. In between the flashes of light, he could barely make out three men from the First Platoon trying to crawl under the amtrac for cover.

Watching the amtracs burn and seeing the three men trying to inch their way under the amtrac, the Lieutenant called out, "No! Not under there! The ammo is still exploding inside!"

But the noise was too intense for anyone to hear. The men ended up burning to death.

In the amtracs, Sergeant Amos led one of Alpha Company's squads; Staff Sergeant Gus Gustafson led the other. Both men were either severely wounded or killed instantly. In the chaos, the Lieutenant wasn't sure which. All the while, ammo continued to explode in loud blasts with white-hot flashes of fire. The Lieutenant kept trying to get through to his company commander on the field radio as he maneuvered the Second Platoon into a position behind the burning amtracs. He wanted the Captain to know the Second Platoon's position and the Lieutenant's plan of action.

"We're coming up behind the amtracs! We'll maneuver to the right of where the amtracs are facing to put us between the wounded and the NVA!" he screamed into the radio.

But the radio was jammed. The Lieutenant and his men fought on. They finally reached Delta Company's line of foxholes. The NVA had jumped into the vacant foxholes and had begun shooting at the Marines. The Marines had the upper hand since they were moving. They fired back at the men, shooting from the foxholes, and maneuvered from foxhole to foxhole, killing off one enemy at a time.

With both A and D Company's dwindling manpower, the Marines were outnumbered by more than four to one. The NVA were coming in waves. They continued pouring into the perimeter. The NVA commanders showed no regard for the lives of their troops. The enemy didn't seem to have any tactical sense. Instead, they just ordered their men to surge forward until they were hit. The Lieutenant had heard about the enemy attacking in constant waves without regard for their casualties, but now he saw it for real.

Gunfire continued until dawn, preventing anyone from getting near the amtracs to retrieve those trapped inside. The NVA used flamethrowers against D Company on the perimeter. Within hours, charred Marine bodies lay strewn across the hill intermingled with the NVA casualties. Although the Marines were outnumbered, the NVA casualties were much higher than that of the Leathernecks.

North Vietnamese fighters rushed toward the Marines from both platoons, carrying Russian-made rifles or carbines. The Lieutenant along with his platoon continued fighting their way from foxhole to foxhole to the north side of the hill firing as they went. They maneuvered under intense gunfire to reinforce Delta Company. The sun was coming up. They could see the amtracs were still on fire. Intermittent ammo explosions blew up inside the amtracs. Casualties for both sides stayed out in the open where no one could get to them because of the intensity of the NVA machine gunfire and the exploding artillery. Wounded cried out in pain for help. The corpsmen did their best to get to the wounded men, as did some of their fellow Marines, but they, too, were fast becoming casualties. Fatalities mounted, but the priority was to kill the NVA inside the perimeter and on the defensive line of Delta Company. The injured simply had to wait. Some continued to scream for help, their voices now hoarse, their pain more desperate.

The Lieutenant directed his men from the two remaining squads of his platoon to cross the landing zone to reinforce Delta Company's perimeter. He led the point man, Lance Corporal Henninger, with his machine gun, along Delta Company's defensive line, to rout out the NVA in D Company's foxholes. The Lieutenant didn't know the location of Delta Company's command bunker, but he led the attack. It was important to reach the command bunker to direct all of the defenses along D Company's line. Captain Corcoran did know, however, where Delta Company's command bunker was, so he came running up to get the Lieutenant and took Henninger off toward the D Company command bunker ahead of the Lieutenant. Captain Corcoran wanted someone with machine gun firepower.

Once the Marines of the Second Platoon secured the command bunker, the tide of battle turned. By then, the Lieutenant had used up all the rounds from his pistol, plus two additional clips of .45 ammo. He reloaded the clips using ammo from a box he carried in his pocket and continued firing at any enemy who drew closer.

The Lieutenant, pistol in hand, along with what was left of his platoon, pressed the attack against the enemy. With their weapons blazing, they ran through a hail of bullets and plodded through a field of bodies. As they continued, some of the platoon members stopped to check the dead NVA. If they were wounded, they carefully disarmed them. It was common knowledge that wounded enemy soldiers often played possum, shot Marines in the back, or set off a hand grenade. The Marines also knew that most of the NVA bodies were booby-trapped.

Still under heavy enemy fire, the Lieutenant and his men worked their way along D Company's defensive line. The Lieutenant then directed his men's gunfire to the north where the NVA had begun retreating.

"Let's keep moving!" he shouted to his men while thrusting his arm forward, motioning to his men where to direct their fire. "Be sure you don't shoot any of our guys from Delta Company!"

The stench of battle came as an entirely separate assault that overpowered the senses. Besides the ever-present smell of cordite that constantly lingered in the blistering air came the powerful smell of blood, the stench of burnt flesh, and the rubber pads burning on the amtracs' tracks. Smoke from the exploded ordnance billowed into the air until it floated up into nothingness.

Finally, the corpsman and the Marines could begin tending to their own wounded. The urgent cry "Doc, over here!" for corpsmen to come get wounded was heard over and over. Somehow the Leathernecks made sure their voices for help on behalf of their buddies were heard above the pandemonium. Several Navy corpsmen, the brave and beloved company docs, lost their lives while treating wounded and tagging deceased bodies.

About this time, as the Lieutenant was wading through Marine bodies, more gunfire erupted from Corporal Alvarez's ambush position. Finally, the Lieutenant managed to get through to him on the field radio,

"This is Alpha Two."

"Fox here," came the reply from Corporal Alvarez. "The enemy is withdrawing right in front of my position!"

"Keep firing!" the Lieutenant yelled.

Corporal Alvarez's squad opened fire. Thirty-two confirmed North Vietnamese soldiers died on the spot. The rest hotfooted it back to their sanctuary north of the DMZ.

After taking up some of Delta Company's positions, the Lieutenant took a few men and retraced his footsteps back to the northeast of Con Thien in the direction where Alvarez and his squad were still firing at the retreating enemy. The gunfire eventually began to settle down some. They passed one NVA who had been gut-shot. His intestines hung out of his body, but he was still alive. The Lieutenant stared down at the man and said, "This guy is no threat to us. One more move and all his organs will spill out. We'll stop on the way back." They passed by him to go after living, moving NVA.

As they zigzagged along, they continued to chase down the enemy, firing as they went, yet only as far as the original ambush position near Alvarez. The Marines could see the NVA were trying to withdraw, but the Lieutenant wanted to maintain gunfire contact to eliminate as many NVA as possible. The remnants of the Marine Second Platoon headed north towards the DMZ. The Lieutenant and his men wanted to chase the NVA all the way north to Hanoi. But Captain Corcoran intervened on the radio and the Lieutenant and his men were ordered to back off from the chase. Corporal Alvarez and his squad linked up with the Second Platoon. The Lieutenant and his men stalked through the area littered with dead and wounded. When they returned, the gut-shot enemy lay dead.

The platoon headed back to Con Thien landing zone. At the landing zone the Lieutenant observed PFC Castro. Somehow, he had miraculously survived the explosion in the amtrac. Castro had been a member of the Lieutenant's Weapons Platoon. The private first class was alive, but bleeding severely from both his ears. His entire upper body was covered in blood and he was clearly in extreme pain. A corpsman was trying to stop Castro's bleeding, but could only bind up his wounds by wrapping his head in bandages. The Lieutenant tried to communicate with Castro, but he was still in shock as he awaited evacuation. It was a huge comfort to know that at least one of his men from the amtrac had survived the seemingly impossible odds. The Lieutenant was glad Castro had lived, and the Lieutenant almost envied him, knowing that Castro would soon be returned to his home in the States. PFC Antonio Castro, from Austin, Texas, was a Marine of excellent character, and one fearless fighter.

Only a few minutes later, the Lieutenant encountered the body of PFC James Huckleberry, another Weapons Platoon member. Huckleberry had fallen next to PFC Nathaniel Johnson, both of whom were killed after they had escaped the doomed amtracs.

The deceased were carefully wrapped in their ponchos. Once again, not enough body bags were available. They'd all been used. As the mortally wounded were being picked up, the Lieutenant came across one of his machine gunners, a teenaged corporal, just nineteen years old, lying face down, lifeless. The Lieutenant stooped over him and lifted him up. When he turned him over, he discovered the man's face was missing. The only way the Lieutenant positively identified the dead man was by his red hair still attached to the back of his remaining skull. Gently, he set him back down and knelt beside him, praying:

"Oh Lord, have mercy on his soul. Receive this young man into Heaven."

The Lieutenant's heart weighed heavily with the loss of his men. He was unable to find any other words to pray.

Whenever possible, the deceased's missing limbs or other body parts were placed near or on top of them. Jeeps and mechanical mules carried fallen Marines from the hilltop to the south side of Con Thien's hill where the medivac choppers could land. Then two men carried each fallen comrade to the medivac helicopters and carefully lined their deceased buddies on the floor.

No matter the number of dead men, the bodies were never stacked. Mortalities were treated with the utmost respect and as much dignity as humanly possible under the circumstances. They were then flown to Dong Ha or Phu Bai, then on to Da Nang for graves registration, and from there, transported to the United States and disbursed to their hometowns for burial. The task of removing the wounded and dead took all day and far into the night.

Combined with the heat, humid air, lack of sleep, continual incoming, loss of life, horrifying cries of the wounded, and the heartbreak of seeing their fellow Marines and Navy corpsman die before their eyes, these accumulated factors left everyone dazed and weary beyond words. The Lieutenant had no outlet to express his rage and grief at the tremendous loss of his men. Stuffing his emotions inside himself was his only alternative. He knew more attacks would continue relentlessly. He needed to maintain his composure in order to lead stoically while motivating his men to fight on.

After the shooting was over, around 0900, the last of the US wounded and fatalities began to be collected. Stretchers were reserved for the wounded. A few moaned in pain. Others shrieked in agony at wounds too horrible to describe. The lucky ones remained unconscious. The Lieutenant wondered how anyone could be alive after all the slaughter around them.

Wounded NVA were also tagged and loaded into helicopters and taken to Dong Ha for triage. Eventually, they were retagged and sent to the rear, perhaps Da Nang, in accordance with the Geneva Convention regulations.

CHAPTER 9

AFTERMATH

MID-MAY 1967

With dawn the next day came flies buzzing over the dead NVA. Their droning sound sickened the Lieutenant. The process of evacuating the dead and wounded seemed endless. Unidentifiable body parts still littered Con Thien's hill. When full daylight arrived, a bulldozer dug a pit in the landing zone, one of the few flat places. The pit stretched about fifteen meters deep and twenty meters long. A small detachment of Marines placed enemy bodies in the hole and covered them up. The enemy death count of left behind men totaled more than two hundred bodies. The enemy's usual practice was to remove the dead and wounded using slaves from the north who had been captured and pressed into service, but this time it was not possible. However, they did manage to carry between two to three hundred deceased back to the DMZ with them.

Many of the dead were the young sappers: children who had never stood a chance. Without weapons, and wearing only underpants, they were buried alongside their slave-master captors. The engineers first inspected all NVA bodies with metal detectors to be sure the bodies weren't booby-trapped. Then they carried them to the pit and placed their bodies in the dirt. Despite the dead being the enemy, none were shown overt disrespect.

Later that morning, the Lieutenant got word of Sergeant Amos' and Staff Sergeant Gustafson's demise. Even though the news wasn't unexpected, the Lieutenant was especially grieved over the loss of Sergeant Amos. He paused, unable to speak, while he tried to gather his thoughts and remember both valiant men as they had been when he last saw them. He felt devastated at their loss, and again, had to stuff down his overwhelming emotions. The Lieutenant remembered at Gio Linh, about a month before, when Sergeant Amos had remarked to him,

"Let's forget all this war foolishness. Let's just go home and see those little boys."

The Lieutenant had wholeheartedly agreed. That was the last conversation the two men ever had.

Why him? He has a wife and a new baby he's never seen. Why are so many good men dying? How can we continue to allow so much destruction of human life? Such a waste. God, why? It isn't fair.

The Lieutenant made a mental note to write Amos' wife. The Lieutenant didn't know her, didn't know her name, and he had never met her. Like himself, Amos must have married soon after the Lieutenant transferred out of Jacksonville.

In the aftermath of the Battle of Con Thien, with so many Marines killed or wounded, Delta Company had to be rebuilt, while Alpha Company had to be reorganized. An entire company from another battalion was trucked in and assigned to replace Delta Company. Those from Delta Company who had survived uninjured were evacuated to Dong Ha for a much needed rest. Alpha Company remained on Con Thien. The First and Third Platoons from A Company suffered the most casualties. The Lieutenant's platoon, the Second, had fewer.

By noon, all dead and wounded had been removed. Between Alpha and Delta Companies, forty-four US Marines had been killed—a blood bath. A brutal, barbaric fight. About 118 US wounded, but fortunately, not all had to be evacuated.

Viewing the carnage of battle, once again, the Lieutenant asked himself, *How is it that any of us lived through this? How did I escape? What have I done to deserve to live? No one can survive this hell. When will my time come? Surely, it's coming soon.*

The fighting continued, though. The Marines still encountered regular artillery gunfire. It seemed to be never-ending. The cumulative number of NVA artillery explosions was estimated to be over two thousand rounds. Occasional rocket fire still came at the Leathernecks as well, but this time from a distance. And for a third consecutive night, no one slept.

By then, the men had hit sensory overload. The sights, smells, sounds, and even the taste in their mouths, along with their sometimes shaking hands, left the men shocked and disoriented, yet they were still willing to fight to the death. The Lieutenant was moved emotionally by their courage and steely determination. Every young warrior had proven himself brave in the face of extreme danger. To a man, all had acted heroically in the Lieutenant's eyes.

The First Platoon's sergeant, Staff Sergeant Burke, had already received relatively minor shrapnel wounds on two separate occasions. In the confusion over the next four days, he was wounded three more times before he was eventually evacuated. The last and most significantly serious wound tore up his hand, but he lived. He was later awarded five Purple Hearts for his multiple wounds. Minor wounds were common for everyone, including the Lieutenant, who'd been hit by shrapnel in the knee during one of the many explosions.

Among the numerous heroic efforts, two men, PFC Finley and Lance Corporal Kreh, proved themselves to be exceptionally brave fighters in the Battle of Con Thien. Finley, a big, loud, swaggering man who packed a side pistol like a cowboy ready for the quick draw, had a personality that reminded the Lieutenant of a playground bully. Kreh, a quiet, no-nonsense man, was pretty much the opposite. Both, however, stepped up as squad leaders by directing their men fearlessly into the hail of gunfire and automatic weapons to rout the NVA from the Delta Company position. Both had died in the battle. The Lieutenant admired their bravery and leadership. Finley, from Illinois, and Kreh, from Michigan, were both recommended for the Navy Cross by the Lieutenant and the surviving witnesses. Finley received his posthumously. Corporal Kreh was awarded the Silver Star posthumously. Later, the Lieutenant wrote up Corporal Alvarez for a Silver Star, which he was awarded.

The fourth day after the battle, from somewhere behind a small makeshift bunker came an awful odor. The smell permeated the area. After a few more days, one of the corpsman found a human femur to be the originating cause. He quickly disposed of the leg, burying it outside the perimeter.

When comparing stories with the other officers, the Lieutenant learned of another particularly scary incident that had happened during the battle of Con Thien. The moment came for Delta Company's commander, Captain John Juul. While Juul was alone in D Company's command bunker on the northwest side of the hill, an enemy soldier burst through the opening, firing his AK-47 assault rifle directly at Juul. However, the enemy's weapon must have been accidentally set for a single shot instead of set on automatic because he only fired once, but Juul fired his .45 pistol simultaneously and killed the intruder. Juul sustained a serious injury, a bullet wound to the upper thigh, and nearly bled out. It was the kind of incident that legends are made of, but Captain Juul lived to tell about it.

The Lieutenant and the remaining platoon sergeants began critiquing the battle. They recorded the sequence of actions and the men's effectiveness in fighting. Additionally, they dissected the wrongs. This took about a half day to sort out. They also had to account for who was dead, who was alive, and where the wounded were located upon evacuation. This proved to be a painful and tedious task.

The worst of the battle was over, but the fighting and shelling still continued.

One of the company drivers moving non-ambulatory wounded men from the open area to a safe place behind the Con Thien hill was Private First Class Del Ray Jacob. His job was to drive up the hill on a mechanical mule, pick up one or two wounded men, drive them back to safety, and then repeat the trip. On one of his trips back, perhaps his third or fourth, he was killed by enemy artillery fire. PFC Jacob was a member of the Lieutenant's Second Platoon.

Del Ray is a residential section of Alexandria, Virginia, near the Lieutenant's hometown. The man with the unique name took pride that he was named for that particular area.

In fact, the Lieutenant had once asked him, "Private, where are you from?"

"Alexandria, Virginia, sir."

"Is that why you're named Del Ray?"

"Yes, sir."

"Well, I wondered. I'm from not very far away, and I know the area well. You have an exceptional name, so be proud of it. "

"I am, sir," the private said with a wide grin.

It was especially hard when a homeboy was killed. Both men were about the same age, and geographically, had grown up very close together. The Lieutenant knew Del Ray Jacob would be buried at Arlington National Cemetery, because his home of record was in nearby northern Virginia. He wished Jacob could have made it home alive. He was a good man and a hard-charging Marine. The Lieutenant felt as though he was running out of places inside himself to store up all his sadness. At some point, he knew he'd start leaking grief. He had no idea how he would cope.

SURFACE TO AIR MISSILE

Back on May 7, the night before the big battle at Con Thien, the Marines on the south side of Con Thien hill heard a jet in the distance, and then watched as a missile shot across the sky towards the plane. They saw one stage of the missile drop off and another fire up, then another. The third stage hit the plane. The last stage had blown the Marine F-4 fighter jet into a million pieces.

In the fireball explosion, several men on the ground swore at the enemy, "Sons of bitches! Where did those shitbird scumbag bastards get their hands on a rocket like that?" someone shouted out.

The answer came three days later on May 10, while the Lieutenant was on a routine patrol of the Con Thien perimeter with his platoon. A squad member from the platoon, Lance Corporal Hogge, stumbled across a seven-foot-long tube-like piece of equipment about two meters in diameter. The metal piece included fins and Russian inscriptions on it. The backward-facing letters in Cyrillic were a dead giveaway.

On the radio, Hogge called to the Lieutenant, "Alpha Two, this is Bear."

"Go ahead, Bear."

"Sir, I've found some equipment you might want to come and see. It's possibly important."

"What's your position?"

In less than three minutes, the Lieutenant had arrived. He knew exactly what the corporal had discovered: a Russian-made surface to air missile (SAM).

"What we've got here is a part of a Russian-made SAM missile," the Lieutenant remarked as he ran his hand over the ordnance. "From these rotating fins, it's probably the guidance part of the missile. I'll bet this is what shot down that fighter jet a couple of nights ago," the Lieutenant reflected. He then added, "Good work, Corporal Hogge."

Hogge, normally a quiet guy who kept to himself, was obviously pleased, but only said, "Just doing my job, sir."

The Lieutenant nodded. "I don't think the US has been able to get their hands on one of these before now. They're usually blown up along with the aircraft they destroy, or else they land in enemy territory. This is an important find, corporal."

The Lieutenant was positive the SAM proved to the allies that Russia was supplying armaments to the North Vietnamese, although they had repeatedly denied it. The Lieutenant radioed his company commander, who advised him, "Leave it there and return to the company position."

But the Captain must have thought better of that order, or perhaps he checked in with his superior, because less than two minutes later, he radioed back.

"Go guard the damn thing until a chopper comes to pick it up. We're not to let it out of our sight."

Everyone got a little squirrely waiting for the helicopter. The platoon of about thirty-plus all realized the constant danger of staying in one place for more than a few minutes without moving. An NVA unit could pick them off at any time. More seriously, they could easily be surrounded and annihilated. Enemy company- and battalion-sized units still roamed the Con Thien area.

Three hours later, a helicopter made contact. It swooped down, dropped a net over the SAM missile, rolled it over, put a hook on it, and flew off, carrying it below. By then dusk had come, and the platoon knew they could possibly be surrounded by the enemy. Wasting no time, they rushed to make it safely back to the company position before darkness fell.

Additionally, it happened that a Marine combat correspondent, who was also an official photographer, had accompanied the platoon on their patrol. He photographed a few of the men standing around the SAM. The Associated Press picked up the picture and story. It ran on the front page of *The Washington Post*, the Lieutenant's hometown newspaper, the following Sunday.

MAY 11, 1967
HELICOPTER CRASH

An American UH -34 helicopter attempted to land on the Alpha Company position on Con Thien to pick up more wounded. The pilot was flying in too high. As he began to slowly descend on the Second Platoon's position, NVA artillery started up again. Men on the ground watched in horror as one of the enemy artillery rounds hit the chopper, causing it to explode in a fireball.

Amazingly, one man survived. The crew chief, a sergeant, happened to be sitting near the side door of the aircraft, so when the explosion occurred, he was blown clear out of the helicopter. He fell down about thirty feet, directly into the Marine's position. Once the shelling stopped, he was medivaced by another helicopter to Dong Ha. Although severely burned, and with multiple broken bones from the fall, he managed to hang on to life. However, the flames had consumed the pilot, co-pilot, and one other crewmember as the helicopter hit the ground in a heap of molten metal. From what remained, all that was identifiable was the engine and the chopper's tail rotor that had blown off in one piece on impact. The incident happened almost directly over the Lieutenant's Second Platoon defensive position—a horrific sight to watch. The men had another close call with death. The Lieutenant felt there was no respite from the May 8 battle.

Still, the shelling continued. On May 13, Alpha Company's commander, Captain Corcoran, suffered multiple wounds to his body from shrapnel from an NVA artillery explosion. The battalion executive officer, Major Boyd, helped the corpsman walk the still conscious Corcoran to a medivac chopper. The Captain wanted the men of Alpha Company, who he commanded, to see him walk. He wanted to die with his boots on. But he didn't die. He was last seen stumbling along with Major Boyd. He was flown out and taken to Dong Ha. Lieutenant Don Campbell, the company executive officer, immediately stepped in and assumed command.

EMERGENCY TRACHEOTOMY

Patrols on Con Thien were a daily fact of life, as were incoming rounds of ordnance. One evening in mid-May, six new replacements showed up around dusk to serve as partial manpower for the Lieutenant's dwindling platoon. Before the Lieutenant had a chance to meet anyone, the Marines in the perimeter were forced yet again to bury their faces in the dust. The swishing sound of incoming rockets caused everyone to drop in place without even having time to dive for their foxholes. Men ate dirt wherever they happened to be.

When the shelling ended, men reached out to check on their neighbors, searching for casualties.

From nearby, came a shout. "Quick! I need some help over here!"

It was the Second Platoon corpsman, Doc Day, who was propping up one of the new replacements. The Lieutenant ran over.

"He's not breathing. His mouth is full of blood!" the corpsman exclaimed. "We've got to act fast! This guy needs a tracheotomy *now*! I don't have any of my equipment with me. What have you got that we can use as a breathing tube?"

The Lieutenant thought for a couple of seconds before he pulled a black US Government ballpoint pen out of his pocket.

"Will this work?" he questioned.

"Yeah, it'll do," the doc replied anxiously.

With shaking hands, the Lieutenant quickly unscrewed the pen and pulled out the ink tube so the black plastic part that had a hole at both ends remained. The doc pulled a penknife from his pocket and made a cut in the man's throat.

"Jam it right here in his neck while I hold him still," the doc said, pointing to the exact spot. The Lieutenant made a couple of stabs to the slit in the man's throat before he succeeded in getting the pen through the cut. Blood spurted on all three men. This should have cleared the airway, but nothing happened. With one arm around the wounded man's back, the corpsman moved him slightly, and that's when the Lieutenant saw that part of the injured man's upper left side was missing. His heart had literally been torn in pieces. He was already dead, undoubtedly, before they'd even attempted to perform the life-saving trach on him.

The Lieutenant sighed. "This man looks to be about eighteen. He just arrived today. I don't even know his name."

"Well," the doc remarked woefully, "We did the best we could for him."

"But he was just a young man. Such a shame. Killed in his first action," the Lieutenant replied with a heavy heart.

The Dark Force had struck again.

USS Iwo Jima

End of Operation Deckhouse VI Phase I at Chu Lai

On the Trace

Installing the Tower at Gio Linh—McNamara's Folly

Doc Day and Staff Sergeant Collins
May 8, 1967, Con Thien with Captured Weapons

SAM Missile: May 10, 1967

Bunker on Operation Cumberland West of Phu Bai, July 1967

Engineers Building a Jungle Hut at Rock-Crusher Site

Daily Dust Storm at Camp Evans

Father Steve Almasy, Church in the Field

Camp Evans

CHAPTER 10

TRANSITION

JUNE 1967

May dissolved into June with hardly anyone noticing. The Second Platoon of Alpha Company still sat on Con Thien. In early June, the Lieutenant received an envelope from the battalion commander, via his company commander.

> On 10 May, the Second Platoon of A/1/4 recovered the guidance section of a SA-2 SAM missile. This item is of significant interest to National Intelligence Agencies. Please convey the following to those officers and men directly responsible for recovery:

> During recent operations, you recovered certain items of NVA equipment of a high technical intelligence interest to the national military authorities. Your attention to duty and alertness are to be commended.

General Wallace M. Greene, Jr.,
US Marine Corps Commandant

A Postscript on the message read "My heartiest congratulations to those whose vigilance made this find possible, Lieutenant General Lewis Walt, Commanding General, Third Marine Amphibious Force."

The Lieutenant wasted no time in sharing this message with the men who had found the SAM, who stood guard with him while they waited for the helicopter to retrieve the missile. Being able to communicate the positive message from both the Commandant and from General Walt's postscript caused the Lieutenant to take additional pride in his men. The men involved beamed with a sense of accomplishment that the commandant himself was aware of their alertness.

Also in early June, the final killed-in-action (KIA) stats for May came in. They showed the devastation from Con Thien on paper. What was written on paper couldn't express the reality of the grief in the hearts of the brave men who lost their buddies. From the battle of Con Thien alone, the May statistics were grim.

May 8, 1967, Battle of Con Thien
(A and D Company)

US Losses	Enemy Losses
4 Officers KIA	197 KIA Confirmed plus
118 men KIA (44 from A Company)	199 KIA Probable
4 Navy Corpsmen (docs) KIA	

These stats represented one official report, but the number was unconfirmed. The Lieutenant knew firsthand that more than two hundred enemy bodies were buried in the pit under the Con Thien landing zone, plus the thirty-two from Alvarez' squad who had been killed. The Lieutenant believed the more accurate number of enemy dead was somewhere between 450 and six hundred.

ANOTHER REORGANIZATION

So many men had been wounded and lives lost during May, that Alpha Company was forced to reorganize leadership at all levels. In the heat of battle, the lack of new replacements grew more critical. The company commander, Captain Corcoran, had been wounded and medivaced on May 13. Additionally, four of the five lieutenants in the company had also been wounded and medivaced. The result was that the enlisted sergeants became platoon commanders.

The Lieutenant retained his place as Second Platoon commander, but also became the company executive officer as an additional responsibility. This position made him second in command under Lieutenant Don Campbell, the new company commander.

Don Campbell, the replacement A company commander, was an eighteen-year Marine veteran who had served in Korea as a private first class. As a senior gunny (gunnery sergeant), he was picked up in May 1966 to be a temporary second lieutenant. His selection as a temporary officer was due to the high number of second lieutenants killed in action in Vietnam.

The Lieutenant had met Don in Okinawa the previous December. After they met, the two Lieutenants often hung out at the bar after hours at Camp Schaub in Okinawa. Eventually, they became friends and were later assigned to the same Company. Don's tour in Vietnam was about half over by then, and he was waiting for his next combat assignment. By the time he took over the company in June 1967, Don was almost ready to finish his tour of duty.

Don Campbell was married, with two teenage daughters. Like many men, he carried his family's pictures with him at all times and showed them to anyone who would look at them.

Don also took a lot of guff from the other lieutenants because of what his dog tags read "no pref," where most tags stated a religious preference (Catholic, Protestant, or Jew) after the Marine's name, rank, serial number, blood type, and marital status. Don hadn't claimed any church affiliation and became the butt of some jokes. The company lieutenants nicknamed him "Lieutenant No Pref" in fun. Don took their teasing good-naturedly.

In the chain of command, after the executive officer came the platoon commanders, all lieutenants. However, all other company officers, except Don and the Lieutenant, had been wounded and evacuated to different areas, depending on the seriousness of their wounds. The result was that senior non-commissioned officers (NCOs), staff sergeants, and above became platoon commanders, an officer's position, and lance corporals became squad leaders, normally a sergeant's position.

The change in leadership became somewhat distressful to the remaining men of the company. Each rifleman had become accustomed to his individual leader. As in March, the men had to adapt to a new chain of command within Alpha Company. They took the changes in their stride, though, and everyone understood his responsibilities. They understood new leadership changed the dynamics of how their unit operated. Men who had previously been following orders became leaders of others. Men had to learn to trust their new leaders. Some of the new leaders adjusted well, and others didn't. The morale of the company depended on the performance of the new leaders, and the acceptance of those leaders by the more junior men. The whole restructuring process was like parents dying and leaving the older kids to step up to raise the family.

During the leadership transition, the relentless shelling continued all around them. Still located on Con Thien's hill, the Lieutenant and his men felt as though they were living like groundhogs, popping up and down in their foxholes. They took incoming fire regularly. Ear-piercing explosions crashed all around them continually. Exhausted and drained of emotion, the men had become accustomed to living on edge. They were grubby and dirt-caked, with bloodshed all around them. They merely existed. They tried to train themselves not to feel, while they constantly attempted to reconcile themselves to imminent death. Deep down, no matter what their religious inclination, the men felt mortality was their ultimate fate.

In the first week of June, the company's daytime priority shifted from defensive positions to providing convoy security from Con Thien to Cam Lo, located six miles away. The Marines rode on trucks, rifles at the ready. They knew they could encounter mines planted in the dirt roadbeds along the way. If a truck hit a mine, everyone knew it meant "Taps." To add to the tension, attacks from NVA RPG rockets, along with machine gunfire, continued as they drove the route. Before nightfall, the men returned to their Con Thien defensive positions, ready to repeat their same nighttime defensive routine.

LIFE AT HOME

On June 7, after some morning shelling, the Lieutenant settled back into his foxhole on Con Thien. In the afternoon, the gunny delivered more letters from home, all dated May. The Lieutenant had a batch from his wife.

May 23, 1967

My darling,

I hope you like the pictures. You'll be glad to know that I had our baby baptized on Sunday afternoon, May 2, and he is officially a junior. Now you have not only a namesake, but also an heir. Everyone says he looks like me, but I think he looks like you. Chuck says he looks like a turnip with ears, but he always has something funny to say!

I bought the baby a white christening outfit for the occasion and wrapped him in the white blanket he got as a shower gift. It was a nice ceremony. Chuck is the godfather and my sister is godmother, as we agreed. Both sets of parents were there, my Aunt Polly, and your sisters.

The baby screamed bloody murder when the priest poured the cold water on his head. I didn't blame the little guy. I wouldn't have liked that either. I didn't know the priest at all, but he seemed nice.

Anyhow, we had a small party at our apartment afterwards with cake and ice cream. I hate it that you are missing this. The pictures don't capture the day, I know, but you get the general idea.

I've carefully packed the christening outfit and blanket away so we can use them again when we

have another son. I miss you so much. The days
drag by without you.

When the Lieutenant finished reading all her letters from the
current batch, he felt like he had failed both his wife and son by not
being there. Encouraged by the reality check of life at home, at the
same time, he felt frustrated and apprehensive about living like an
animal in his foxhole. Life continued to be a two-edged sword. Her
letters were all he had to look forward to. Without them, he knew
he would give up.

MORE FIGHTING

On one occasion in the early days of June, instead of convoy duty,
Alpha Company was assigned to carry out its last mission near Con
Thien, at least temporarily. Orders arrived to clear an area on the
east side of the road south of the Con Thien hill.

Along the way, the men of Alpha Company encountered about
fifty NVA who had dug in defensive positions and bunkers not far
from Con Thien. Initially, the First and Second Platoons began the
attack towards the southeast of the Con Thien perimeter.

Less than a mile out, Alpha Company engaged in a firefight
with the NVA. Don, the company commander, ordered the First
Platoon to start shooting at the enemy to pin them down where
they were and distract them from any maneuver to surround them.
The Second Platoon, led by the Lieutenant, was ordered to go
around to the enemy's left flank to attack their position.

Staff Sergeant Collins of the Second Platoon was the point man.
He stormed the NVA bunkers with a machine gun and with a squad

of twelve Marines behind him. Collins, a little over six feet tall, was known to be an aggressive attacker and a bear of a man. He was fierce with a machine gun, and he terrified the NVA. Most looked at him as if he were a giant. They turned tail and ran. The Marines pursued the enemy for about two hundred yards and then stopped, so as not to get drawn into a trap. Later, when the company returned to their positions at Con Thien, the men hoped to be able to get some to rest. Instead, they were met with another barrage of artillery from the NVA, and the Marines ended up returning fire for the next three hours.

One artillery round struck the edge of Corporal Sander's foxhole. The impact caused dirt to fall on top of him and he was buried alive. Miraculously, neither the explosion nor any shrapnel pieces wounded him. The wet ground, from the almost daily rainfall, had absorbed the majority of the impact. His buddies dug him out in a hurry. He spit dirt and wiped the mess out of his eyes, ears, and nose. Still, he remained dazed for a few hours afterwards.

The Lieutenant could see he was severely traumatized and could not stop shaking. The Lieutenant insisted, over Corporal Sanders' protests, that he be medivaced. The corporal was returned fit for duty after a few days of recovery.

Days later, new orders moved Alpha Company off Con Thien to an area south of C-2, a defensive position fortified with bunkers and artillery, just north of Cam Lo. Cam Lo is located at the intersection of the north/south road to Con Thien and Route 9, an east/west road from Dong Ha to Khe Sanh.

ALIENS

In two more days, Alpha Company moved again, this time to the south to await transport to Camp Evans. The Leathernecks camped along a stream where the men could rest in relative safety. The area where they rested was known as Leatherneck Square, an approximate square area including Con Thien, Cam Lo, Gio Linh, and Dong Ha. After five long weeks, the men could wash in the stream and have a little peace and quiet away from the fighting. Before reaching the stream, all the Marines, no matter their skin color, appeared to have been dyed orange, the result of spending weeks crawling through the dirt and dust without any opportunity to bathe. The Lieutenant thought everyone looked like aliens.

After several days rest, the company was moved by truck convoy from Leatherneck Square to Camp Evans, farther south.

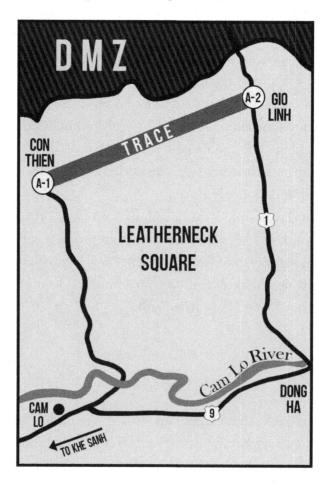

MID-JUNE 1967
CAMP EVANS

Alpha Company now temporarily relocated to Camp Evans, the headquarters of the Fourth Marine Regiment. Situated south of Dong Ha, it was halfway between Dong Ha, Hue City, and Phu Bai. Unlike Con Thien, Camp Evans was out of reach of NVA artillery and rockets. The camp, a tent city, looked like an administrative rest area, but was in fact, an operational base. Although there were no bunkers in sight, the camp remained fortified with defensive positions and surrounded by barbed wire. The camp was a base from which outposts were established to keep the enemy from massing attacks on Phu Bai or Hue City.

After weeks of eating C-rations, the returning men from A Company finally got hot food and cold showers. The shower, a rigged up fifty-five-gallon drum, was placed atop a ten-foot-high tower with a pull chain to release the water. The shower provided some cool refreshment from the intense heat. Each company had one and sometimes two shower drums. Men stood naked in line waiting for a splash of cold water.

On their first evening, the men feasted on a full meal, and were delighted to find a treat of fresh strawberries on the menu for dessert. Fresh fruit of any kind was a rarity in Vietnam. The men ate heartily.

Initially, Alpha Company took up the perimeter defense for Camp Evans. Then the First Platoon was ordered to go out and establish a patrol base on Hill 51, a few miles southwest of Camp Evans. The base overlooked the Co Bi Than Tan Valley. Several days later, another platoon, the Third, along with the company command post whose personnel included the Lieutenant as company executive officer, joined the First Platoon on Hill 51. Additionally, four tanks were attached to Alpha Company on Hill 51. While occupying Hill 51, a firefight erupted with small arms. It was there that the Lieutenant stood too close to an M60 tank as it shot off a round. The sound reverberated through his head. It felt like a spike being driven through his ear. The muzzle blast from the firing tank caused him to permanently lose most of the hearing in his left ear. It also caused a loud ringing in both ears, resulting in permanent tinnitus.

The Cobi Tan Than Valley was saturated with booby traps and mines, including 250-pound bombs rigged with trip wires. One afternoon, a man from Alpha Company, a private first class, accidentally stumbled onto a trip wire and the enemy bomb detonated. He was instantly killed. As point man for his squad, he led the maneuver. He knew it was a high-risk position. He would have been the first to encounter either booby traps or the enemy face to face. The point position rotated periodically because of the stress involved.

Miraculously, no one else was killed in the same explosion. At least the man suffered little to no pain. However, the effect of such instant loss substantially raised the tension of the entire First Platoon. After evacuating the private's remains, the patrol continued their maneuver as mapped out until the evening, when they returned to the Hill 51 perimeter. Although the deceased Marine was not from the Lieutenant's platoon, the Lieutenant was once again saddened by the news of the casualty from another random mine explosion.

LIEUTENANT NO PREF GOES HOME

A little before mid-June, First Lieutenant Don Campbell, still the acting company commander who'd replaced Captain Corcoran, finally came to the end of his tour. Don—Lieutenant No Pref—left for home in San Diego. The Lieutenant was sorry to see Don go, but was glad Don had finished his tour in one piece. After saying their goodbyes, the two men agreed to stay in touch.

When fresh replacements finally arrived at Camp Evans during the third week of June, Captain George Stern replaced Don. As second senior officer in Company A (after Captain Stern), the Lieutenant became company executive officer permanently by default. He actually had outranked Campbell. He could have been the temporary company commander instead of Don, but preferred to do double duty by retaining command of the Second Platoon as well as acting as the company executive officer. This was the Lieutenant's preference. He was keenly aware that this would most likely be his only chance to command a platoon in combat, and he coveted the chance. He felt genuinely dedicated to his men. But if he had taken temporary duty as the company commander, he would have been out of daily contact with his platoon. In truth, there weren't enough officers and senior NCOs to go around. With so many casualties and deaths, each battalion was stretched to the limit for personnel of any rank. Vacancies were critical. Captain Stern didn't last long. He was a short-timer, and due to rotate back to the States within about six weeks. The Lieutenant disliked the practice of inserting company commanders for such a short period of time. He found it disruptive to everyone in the company. Captain Stern's replacement was Captain Keith Thompson, who would retain command of the company for the next six months.

JUNE 13, 1967
ANNIVERSARY

When the mailbag arrived again, the Lieutenant received a flowery anniversary card from his wife. Mushy and sweet, the words on the card made him feel alone and empty inside. It was dated June 4, one week prior to June 11, their first wedding anniversary. She wrote that she hoped it would arrive on time. It was only two days late, but the Lieutenant didn't mind. He had been so preoccupied that he hadn't sent her any anniversary greetings, which made him feel terrible. He hoped she would understand.

Married a full year? In some ways it seems like yesterday, and in other ways, it seems like an eternity ago.

He reminisced about the June night in 1964 when they became engaged. Coming home from a date, he had pulled the car over to the side of the road and proposed. She said yes right away. He'd saved for weeks to afford the diamond ring. She said the ring was exactly what she'd always wanted. They celebrated by going for a long walk, holding hands and planning their future. He remembered the rush of elation he felt at the anticipation of spending their lives together. He had never felt this happy before. He enjoyed the feeling of contentment that they were lost in their own little world. June was her favorite month of the year, he remembered. She said how much she enjoyed the soft breezes and sweet smell of honeysuckle. She loved the promise of summer, and she loved him. He was a happy man.

Days after they became engaged, the Lieutenant was off to boot camp at Parris Island. Her dad wouldn't okay the wedding until the Lieutenant, then a private, made sergeant (E-5). They were determined to wait. Her dad wanted to be sure he earned enough money for them to live on. All that changed, though, when he received orders to Officer Candidate School (OCS). It was two years after boot camp when they finally married. June turned out to be the perfect month for their wedding. It came right after the Lieutenant had completed OCS, and just days prior to him beginning the next phase of officer training, The Basic School. On his lieutenant's salary, they thought they were rich. With her paycheck added in, it seemed like they were rolling in money. They had more than enough to get by on.

The Lieutenant stared at the card in his hands and at her signature. He could picture her sitting at their little round dining table, addressing the envelope to him. How nice that the envelope and card were clean and dainty, not covered in dirt like everything south of the DMZ. She had drawn little hearts with arrows going through them all over the bottom of the card. She signed with x's and o's. Her letters seemed like the only normal thing he knew.

Their wedding had taken place on a sunny Saturday morning in June. She looked like a princess in her white wedding gown. She glowed as her father walked her down the aisle. He wore his white summer dress uniform. The church was filled with family and friends, and the couple laughed as they ran down the aisle arm in arm after the ceremony. For the reception, there were hors d'oeuvres, cake, and champagne. The Lieutenant cut the cake using his grandfather's Marine ceremonial sword. The reception wasn't much, but they were short on time; he had to be on the Rifle Range at Quantico at 0630 the following Monday morning. His bride drank a little too much champagne at the reception and giggled a lot before they left, but not so much that anyone really noticed. How they laughed driving away from their party! They both felt like they had pulled off a great coup. They did it! They were married! They were beginning a great adventure together. The Lieutenant's pal, Joe, put a big hand-lettered "Just Married" sign on the back of the Lieutenant's pea green '62 Ford Falcon. People honked their horns at them as they drove down the road. The couple waved back, still laughing. It was all a big lark. They were drunk on love. Later that night, at a restaurant, the Lieutenant put away a steak dinner with all the trimmings, while his bride sat demurely eating a scoop of vanilla ice cream. She had no appetite. The booze had upset her stomach earlier and she wound up tossing her cookies.

The Lieutenant laughed out loud at the thought. But his laughter almost turned to tears. *If only I could see her. If only I could eat another steak dinner.*

They never had time for a honeymoon. They had only a few precious months together before his deployment. The Lieutenant resented being robbed of so much happiness away from his wife and infant son. He felt disgust with the war and with the chaos of the country. But most of all, he despised the politicians who he blamed for the mess they had created in Vietnam.

NEWBIE GETS LOST

Around the end of June, Alpha Company was ordered to become part of Operation Cumberland, the next in series of operations. The company moved to the area east of the A Shau Valley. They were to provide security for two batteries of US Army 175mm self-propelled cannons, the largest in the US artillery arsenal. For the remainder of the month, A Company encountered only sporadic small arms fire and 82mm mortar attacks from the NVA while they patrolled the area they were guarding. Thankfully, no KIAs. Only a few minor wounded in actions were reported.

By the end of June, all the platoons in Alpha Company were receiving fresh replacements. First, the Lieutenant commanded the Weapons Platoon, later the Second Platoon, then simultaneously was acting executive officer and Second Platoon commander. Finally, he was moved into the permanent company executive officer's slot. It was considered a promotion for him. Now the Lieutenant's job was to devote his full time and attention to being the executive officer for the entire company. He was not pleased. He would rather not be stuck with administrative duties; he wanted to be with his men. There was one perk, however; he got to sleep inside a tent on a cot in the rear at Camp Evans. The downside was that he shared the tent with nine other snoring men.

He got a wooden footlocker, the beat-up kind he could sign out from supply, and placed it at the foot of his cot in the general-purpose sleeping tent. It would have to be turned in when he left the position, but it worked to keep his belongings dry in the meantime. A willy peter bag (WP, or waterproof bag) placed inside the trunk held those items he especially wanted to keep out of the damp, muggy climate.

His replacement, the new Second Platoon commander, was a brand new second lieutenant just out of The Basic School in Quantico. On the afternoon of his first combat patrol outside the artillery base, he drifted along with his entire platoon too far from the base perimeter. He lost his bearings in the thick vegetation of the surrounding hills. His platoon was never in any danger, but he became disoriented. He could not find his way back to the perimeter.

He radioed in for directions. Unfortunately, the radio traffic between the new lieutenant and the new company commander, Captain Keith Thompson, was picked up by the Battalion Combat Operations Center. They relayed the information to the Regimental Combat Operations Center.

At this point, the battalion commander, Lieutenant Colonel Deptula, and the regimental commander, a full colonel, got involved in attempting to reorient the lieutenant. The newbie was trying to respond to his company commander, the battalion commander, and the regimental commander all at once.

To make matters even worse, at that very moment, General William C. Westmoreland of the US Army, the four-star Commander in Chief of all US forces in Vietnam, the big kahuna himself, happened to be flying over the immediate area in his private helicopter.

Westmoreland was there to observe Operation Cumberland. He heard all the commotion on the radio traffic, and he directed his helicopter pilot to begin searching for the lost platoon.

The lieutenant was sitting back at the base camp, along with Alpha Company's commander, Captain Thompson. They were monitoring the radio traffic.

The Lieutenant remarked to the Captain, "Westmoreland oughta go back to Saigon. It's no wonder we're losing this war. That guy does not need to be micro-managing second lieutenants. The new lieutenant and his men are not in any danger."

"You've nailed it!" Captain Thompson agreed. "I think Westmoreland's out of his league. The lieutenant needs to work his way out of his problem and get back to the perimeter. He should to do this on his own. How else is he going to learn? Better that he learns it here than when we're back up at the DMZ."

Eventually, everyone, including the brass, backed off and left the problem for the new lieutenant to solve by himself. Early the next morning, the newbie lieutenant returned unscathed, along with his men. Unfortunately for him, because of all the high-ranking interference, he was relieved of his duties to become the SLJO (Shitty Little Jobs Officer) somewhere in the battalion rear. The Lieutenant felt like the guy was a good man, but never had the chance to redeem himself.

CHAPTER 11
ADMIN

EARLY JULY 1967

As of July first, the Lieutenant received a promotion to first lieutenant. The gold bar insignia on his collar was replaced with a silver bar. His commanding officer, Captain Thompson, pinned the new rank insignia on his uniform, as was customary, and handed him a certificate. The promotion was SOP (standing operating procedure). There was a salute and a congratulatory handshake; that was all.

Now company executive officer, the Lieutenant bunked at Camp Evans. His time would be divided between Camp Evans, Phu Bai and Operation Cumberland, a fluid and ongoing campaign. He wasn't particularly pleased with the new arrangement. He didn't want to be stuck in a tent doing administrative duties.

The following day, the Lieutenant received a Red Cross message from the States concerning Sergeant Junior L. Schriner, the Second Platoon guide in Alpha Company, a man the Lieutenant knew well. Summoned from the perimeter defense at Camp Evans, the Lieutenant took Schriner into an adjacent tent, where it was relatively private, and informed him,

"I regret to tell you that we received a message from your family that your brother has passed away. It was an accidental drowning two days ago."

The sergeant put his hands over his face in disbelief and horror. He began to weep softly.

The Lieutenant waited for a few minutes while Schriner absorbed this information before he continued quietly.

"I'm so sorry; I know this is quite a shock. It's a lot to absorb. We'll make immediate arrangements for your emergency leave for whatever time you need to be with your family. Go get your gear together and stay in the company area until we can get you to Phu Bai to process out. The company driver will take you there by Jeep. If possible, we'll get you out of here within the next few hours."

Two hours later, Sergeant Schriner left for his home in Virginia. Schriner was a deeply serious man who took his responsibilities to heart and could be depended upon to do the right thing. The men of the Second Platoon respected him. The Lieutenant trusted Schriner to return to Vietnam in a timely manner, despite his personal loss.

JULY 4, 1967
FIREWORKS

At Camp Evans on the Fourth of July, about the time it got dark, some of the Lieutenant's men from the office helped themselves to a box of illumination flares. These were readily available all around the perimeter to light up the area if attacked by the NVA. The men began setting them off without any authorization. Flares were hand-held. Just pull the cap off the top, twist the cylinder on the bottom, hold it up and out, Statue-of-Liberty style, wait for the pop sending it up in the air, then watch the bursting flash of white light and see it drift down like a little parachute illuminating the night sky.

They had a high time, hooting and hollering in celebration. More men joined the fun. Pretty soon some of the men from the support perimeter joined in, then more troops from the Second Battalion, Fourth Marines showed up. In no time, there were hundreds of flares floating down from the sky. The whole camp was lit up!

The Lieutenant figured the men deserved a little entertainment, especially on Independence Day, so he just sat back and watched the action, amused. He was pleased they had found a diversion from the routine.

Then a corporal found him and reported, "Sir, the regimental commander wants to see you right away."

Shit, the Lieutenant thought. *He's gonna have my butt in a sling for this.*

He knew a reprimand was coming, so he took his time walking the fifty meters to the battalion headquarters tent. According to protocol, before reporting to the regimental commander, he had to check in first with the battalion commander. Besides, he wanted the men to have as much time as possible to celebrate.

When he got to the battalion headquarters, instead of reporting to the colonel, the regimental commanding officer, he was met by the battalion executive officer, Major Mike Sheridan, who told him, "Don't worry. We've put the Old Man back to bed. I'll handle him. Let the men have their fun, but you must contain it."

"Yes, sir!" The Lieutenant saluted and left, grateful for not getting chewed out. It took about twenty minutes of yelling, "Cease fire! Cease fire!" But by then the men had just about stopped.

Everyone knew they were in no danger from giving away their position to the enemy. The NVA knew exactly where they were, but couldn't reach them with their fire power. It had been a great way for the troops to let off a little steam.

JULY 5, 1967
DERELICTION

The next day, the Lieutenant was sitting at a field desk at Camp Evans inside a general-purpose tent that substituted for the company office. He opened the deep bottom-desk drawer and found personal items: watches, wallets, a small Bible, some letters, and a few other odds and ends. These items were obviously all personal effects of deceased Marines. On closer examination, he discovered two of the items were Sergeant Amos' Bible and wallet. He was furious to realize that after two months, these items still hadn't been inventoried, processed, or forwarded to the next of kin. This was the responsibility of the company first sergeant (E-8), who had seriously neglected his duty.

The Lieutenant spent the next few hours taking care of this chore himself. When he brought the first sergeant, a crusty, older WWII veteran, up for questioning, his only excuse was, "I forgot, sir."

"I don't give a rat's ass what you forgot!" the Lieutenant barked. "I could have you court-martialed for this, you maggot!

Those brave men died in battle and depended on you to see that their belongings were sent home. Your job is to ensure that all personal effects are mailed to the next of kin as soon as possible, not left lying around in a bottom drawer somewhere! You have not done your job, and you know it! This is clearly dereliction of duty. Be assured, your next fitness report will reflect your conduct. Dismissed," the Lieutenant snapped.

The term "maggot" is traditionally applied to new recruits at Parris Island when they arrive for basic training. What the first sergeant would have heard was the Lieutenant emotionally and metaphorically stripping him of his rank.

The first sergeant, usually not one to show facial expressions, barely concealed a disdainful smirk as he left the command tent.

Normally, senior NCOs command respect from junior officers. However, there were exceptions, and the Lieutenant felt this was one of those times. So many senior NCOs had been called up for duty in Vietnam and killed over the past two years. Other NCOs had declined the offer of temporary commissions, as this first sergeant had done. Still others had taken temporary commissions or been sent to Officer Candidate School to become permanent officers. It was possible for someone like the Lieutenant, who had been a corporal E-4 only a year earlier, to outrank a senior NCO the following year. This situation regarding former enlisted men becoming officers made for some jealousy, as well as awkward moments. However, the Lieutenant felt justified in his enraged response to this particular senior NCO.

The Lieutenant knew, too, that the smirking first sergeant was just biding his time. He had twenty-five years in the Corps, and was looking forward to retirement when his tour of duty was up in a few weeks. Court-martialing him would have served no purpose. Instead, the Lieutenant wrote a scathing fitness report that would ensure the sergeant would never see another promotion while serving on active duty. Pointless, since the first sergeant planned to retire, but at least the last fitness report would follow him into civilian life.

FIRST SERGEANT CRAWFORD

When the first sergeant left a week or so later, his replacement was First Sergeant (E-8) Leland D. Crawford, the complete antithesis of the man who'd just departed. Crawford was one superlative Marine who later became the Sergeant Major of the Marine

Corps. This prestigious position, the highest-ranking enlisted man in the entire Marine Corps, made him the enlisted equivalent of the commandant.

The Lieutenant quickly realized that Sergeant Crawford didn't like admin any more than he did. Crawford, too, wanted to be with the troops in the field. Unlike the former first sergeant, Crawford always chose to be alongside the men whenever possible.

"Well, Lieutenant, I've got to get back out in the field to see the troops. Why don't you take a turn babysitting the office and supply people for a change?" he asked lightly. Crawford asked this so often that the question became a running joke between the two men.

"That's okay. You go," the Lieutenant always answered. "I'll be relieving you in the field in a couple of days anyway."

The Lieutenant also wanted to be with his men in the field. He missed the action, so he visited the troops whenever he could. His reply to Sergeant Crawford served to let him know that the Lieutenant had no intention of staying put in the field office for any length of time, either.

Whereas the former first sergeant couldn't name more than ten guys in the company, Crawford learned the names of every man in the company. Crawford also proved himself a worthy Marine by going on patrol with the men. He'd pick up a rifle and go on day patrols, night patrols, anything. He would allow corporals and sergeants much lower in rank than he to do their job of leading others. Crawford even took orders from them—something that shocked the junior NCO leaders. Because of this, the men loved him and admired him. The Lieutenant and Sergeant Crawford worked well together. They enjoyed a great rapport and each respected the other.

MID-JULY 1967
BLACK MARKET AND OTHER SIGHTS

In mid-July, and on the move once more, the First Battalion, Fourth Marine Regiment was trucked to Phu Bai to be airlifted to Dong Ha to begin another operation. Yet for some unknown reason, the flights were canceled, and the entire battalion was trucked all the way to Dong Ha instead. This took the better part of the day. The Lieutenant followed in a company Jeep driven by a private.

While he bumped along the road, riding shotgun, the Lieutenant enjoyed a smoke as he looked around at the countryside. It felt good not to be riding in a helicopter, even if the journey did take longer. The convoy traveled on Route 1, the only paved road in the region. They passed through Hue City and a number of villages along the way. Hue City dated back more than two thousand years and was the former location of the emperor more than a thousand years ago. Called the Imperial City, Hue became an important symbol for the unification of North and South Vietnam. It held the potential for a major battle because many sympathizers, both north and south, re-sided there. It was destined to become a major battleground in only a few months. Driving through Hue, the ancient Imperial Palace and Citadel could be seen in the old part of the city. Some streets were paved. The city bustled with small cars, motor scooters, and a few rickshaws pulled by men wearing conical straw hats.

As the convoy drove on, the Lieutenant knew that going north to Dong Ha meant going right back to Leatherneck Square and the many unseen dangers that lurked there. He felt like he lived on a treadmill with no end to the fighting in Vietnam.

Will this time near the DMZ be like the last? Will it be like in March, April, May, and June, when we were involved in such heavy fighting and so many were killed? The summer had been relatively slow so far, with only sporadic action. Yet he questioned whether he had it in himself to go through all the terror and heartache again.

I just want to go home and be with my wife. I want to get the hell out of Vietnam. I want to see our baby. I wonder what he'll look like. Pictures are one thing, but having a real live baby to hold in my arms is different.

As the battalion moved farther along Route 1, the Lieutenant saw small villages not far off the road, and he knew the farmers and their families were relatively safe.

They live in their little grass huts, working in the fields and in the rice paddies all day. Their lives seem so simple, but they also work hard. I wonder if they know or even care about this war, or the violence and death that surround them. What will they do when the US troops are gone?

Route 1 was an area noted for its black market shops. Small stands seemed to have sprung up everywhere, like spring weeds, selling anything and everything the Marines couldn't get anywhere else. For instance, with C-rations, the men were issued just four individual cigarettes per container. The black market, however, had cartons of US cigarettes for sale—of course, at greatly inflated prices. Also, the black market traders sold American-made whiskey, not available anywhere else in the northern I Corps area. Beer was sold, too, along with imported US food items, such as candy bars, junk food, and other desirable snacks unavailable to anyone. Clothes and watches were also big on the black market. It was obvious they were all US products, marked with US stamps. None of the US post exchanges in the northern I Corps area of South Vietnam carried such a variety of goods.

It was forbidden for Americans to do business with these Vietnamese profiteers, so the majority of their patrons were the American staff "pogues," the paper-shuffling types. "Pogues" was the name given to American military personnel, US civilians who worked near the big bases, and for the local Military Assistance

Command, Vietnam (MACV) compounds dotting Route 1. The staff people got all the luxuries, while the troops got all the garbage. This was how it worked: The black market accepted cash only. American money. And most of the payments were military payment certificates (MPCs). Buyers paid for the goods with MPCs in denominations of one-, five-, ten-, or twenty-dollar increments. MPCs were just like American greenbacks, but because the US Government didn't want greenbacks infiltrating Vietnam, they developed the MPC system. Items were marked up. When black market merchants got a hold of MPCs, they sold them for twice their printed value. The black market guys were profiteering not only from the locals, but also from the US servicemen who were doing the fighting.

JULY 14-16, 1967
OPERATION HICKORY II

Operation Hickory II ran concurrently with Operation Cumberland. Hickory included five Marine infantry battalions, about five thousand men. The purpose was to attack NVA positions between the Cam Lo River and Con Thien hill. This large-scale operation was conducted under the control of the Ninth Marine Regiment. Battalions and companies were often temporarily reassigned to different regimental control. It was extremely unusual for so many battalions to be deployed in so small an area. Temporary attachments, like one in which the Lieutenant's battalion participated, made the Lieutenant feel the frustration of not being able to maintain unit cohesion in battle—an essential in war.

After intense fighting, the enemy was routed out and driven north of the DMZ once again. Unfortunately, the Lieutenant remained behind at Dong Ha performing administrative duties and feeling as though he was missing a significant battle. His entire being told him he should be with his company, not sitting this one out in the rear.

Being shifted to staff duty feels like a betrayal to my troops in Alpha Company. They never get a break from being riflemen, while platoon commanders like myself only get to command for a few months before being reassigned.

The immediate area of Operation Hickory II bordered on the trace near Con Thien. This was the same place that the First Battalion, Fourth Marines had cleared earlier that year. Since that time, the area had become pockmarked with bomb and artillery craters. To the Lieutenant, the area looked like pictures of the moon's surface—bleak, dismal, and devoid of any vegetation. The area was littered with abandoned NVA weapons and other military equipment, including metal debris from explosions, and even some clothing remnants.

Although no one got a snapshot of it, one of the platoon leaders saw a crater at the trace with a hand sticking out of the side of one of the holes. It reminded everyone who saw it of a scene from a horror flick, like a hand coming up from the grave. The hand belonged to the enemy—the Marines would not have left any body part out in the open. This grotesque sight repulsed the Lieutenant and everyone who saw it or heard about it.

Operation Hickory II lasted until July 16, when the First Battalion, Fourth Marine Regiment was again trucked to Camp Evans. Everyone, including the Lieutenant, felt more than ready for a few days away from the noise and chaos of combat at the DMZ.

CHAPTER 12

IGNORING REGULATIONS

MID- TO LATE JULY 1967

In the Marine Corps, casualty death notices were stringently restricted to official channels. The casualty notification process had to remain within the official channels, no matter the cause of death or the relationship the unit commander had with the deceased. Although forbidden, it was not uncommon for platoon or company commanders to write letters outside the official channels to a deceased Marine's next of kin. Officially, all communication was initiated, reviewed, and signed by either the battalion commander or regimental commander only after the battalion adjutant had drafted the initial death notification. Then, the notice was formally sent by wire to Headquarters Marine Corps in Washington, DC. From there, headquarters would schedule a personal visit by a Marine casualty call officer, along with a Navy chaplain, to the next of kin. This visit generally took place a short time after the death or wounding of a Marine, usually within twenty-four hours. A follow-up telegram would also be issued. However, members of the Marine's individual units had strict orders never to communicate personally with any next of kin.

In one case, however, the Lieutenant felt obligated to ignore the order. Sergeant Floyd Amos, who the Lieutenant knew from his time in Jacksonville and who died in the amtrac on May 8 in the battle of Con Thien, was an exception. It had been two months since Sergeant Amos' death, but the Lieutenant hadn't forgotten his resolve to write the widow. He had already mailed Amos' personal effects back to Florida on July 5, but he felt a personal letter would be appropriate. The Lieutenant was sure Mrs. Amos knew of him, and he also knew their sons had been born on the same day.

Screw the rules, he thought.

Writing letters of any kind did not come easily to the Lieutenant. His letters to his own wife were usually just one short page. He just couldn't think what to say. It was difficult for him to express his grief. He wished he could be better at saying how badly he felt about the death of Floyd Amos. He struggled to find the right words. He rewrote the letter numerous times before finally settling.

July 17, 1967

Dear Mrs. Amos,

I am writing this letter to express my sincere sympathy to you and your family for your loss of Floyd. As you know, we were friends during our time at the Marine barracks in Jacksonville. His bravery and heroism during battle reflected well on him as an outstanding Marine and a well-respected leader. Please feel free to contact me if I can answer any questions.

Almost two weeks later her reply arrived.

July 29, 1967

Dear Lieutenant,

Thank you for your letter and for making contact with me. Thank you, too, for sending Floyd's
wallet, Bible, watch, and other belongings. I will
always treasure them.

I haven't received any information regarding his
death since the official notice when the chaplain
and the casualty call Marine showed up at my
house. Could you tell me specifically how my
husband died? Was he in pain? Any other information you can share would be so appreciated. I
want to know as many specific details as you can
give me.

Yours Truly

Again, the Lieutenant tried to find the right words in his return
letter.

How could he tell a loved one how truly awful it had been?
How could he tell the truth, but not exaggerate or understate? How
could he share personal condolences without sounding trite? What
words could he use to express how deeply he had been affected by
the death?

July 31, 1967

Dear Mrs. Amos,

This is what I know regarding your husband's final moments. We were all under attack at Con Thien. The battle was intense. He was part of the reinforcement at the defensive perimeter. The amphibious tractor he was riding in was struck multiple times by rocket fire. The tractor exploded and only a few men were able to get out. He was severely wounded, and never regained consciousness. It is my understanding that he died before being medically evacuated. It all happened very quickly.

Once again, I want to assure you that Floyd was an outstanding Marine and well respected by those who knew him. We all share in your grief. He was a good friend to me, as well.

Sincerely

CONSIDERING R&R

Every Marine stationed in Vietnam during the conflict was entitled to five days rest and relaxation (R&R) to be taken out of the country. The only qualification was that the serviceman had served in-country for at least six months. If the Marine chose to take his R&R nearby, like in Thailand or Taiwan, or even Australia, then he was only granted three days leave. Many Marines, however, chose

Hawaii as their R&R destination. For Hawaii, they were granted five days, thereby giving them two days travel time.

The Lieutenant had firmly decided not to take R&R. He was dead set against it. He had seen what had happened to others. Men lost their focus before leaving, but mostly after returning from R&R. Before leaving, men daydreamed about getting out of Vietnam, but returning to the civilian world disoriented them. The shock of being transported by jet from foxhole living to resort utopia, in a matter of just hours, overwhelmed most men. R&R lasted only a few days, but it was an adjustment most couldn't make. Whenever men saw the normal civilian way of life again, they longed to become part of it once more. They lost the rhythm of day-to-day warfare. Returning to the battlefield after R&R proved equally traumatic to most. Too many men wound up getting killed. It was a pattern the Lieutenant had often observed over the previous months. The Lieutenant didn't want to take that kind of a chance for just five days.

His wife had already written about her friend who was met by the casualty call officer and the Navy chaplain as soon as she deplaned for R&R in Oahu. Her husband of less than one year was dead, killed by a sniper. The Lieutenant had long since made it clear to his wife his choice not to go to Hawaii. He suspected she didn't really understand his decision.

During July, a letter arrived from her begging him to meet her in Hawaii when he got his R&R. She'd saved enough money for the trip, and her friends who had gone had come back with glowing reports.

"Wouldn't it be possible to plan this? Please," she pleaded.

After reading her letter, he relented and wrote back for her to begin making plans for the trip. He gave her dates in September when he would be able to get leave to travel to Hawaii. He'd decided to take his chances. He desperately wanted to see her, if only for a few days.

She'd written back that she felt her biggest decision regarding the trip revolved around whether she should bring the baby or leave him with the Lieutenant's mother. He would be six months old by then, and she felt really torn. She was so proud of their son and wanted her husband to meet him. They both knew it could possibly be the only time he'd ever see his son. But she questioned whether it was prudent to bring the child all the way from the East Coast. It would disrupt the baby's schedule for days. On one hand, the Lieutenant earnestly wished to see his son; but his son was an unknown, a strange concept he just couldn't get his head around. On the other hand, he felt fearful not to see the baby in case he himself didn't survive. He just didn't know what to do. He couldn't decide, so he left it up to his wife. In the end, she opted to leave the child at home and hoped she'd made the right decision.

SERGEANT'S RETURN

Late in July, Sergeant Schriner, the man whose brother had drowned, returned from emergency leave and reported back to Alpha Company. He again took up his duties as platoon guide. Almost immediately, the Lieutenant worried for his morale. As the Lieutenant had previously observed, once men went away for various reasons such as injury, emergencies at home, or R&R, they appeared to be distracted and their attention diverted when they returned. Many became careless after they came back. This seemed to be the case with Schriner, and it was worrisome. The Lieutenant hoped Schriner would readjust quickly. There wasn't much the Lieutenant could do for the sergeant, except keep an eye on him.

PHU BAI
MEETING OLD PALS

At the end of the month, during Operation Cumberland, the Lieutenant happened to be in Phu Bai on administrative business as part of his new role as executive officer. While he walked from one jungle hut to another, he literally ran into Jack Wolpe, a private first class from the barracks in Jacksonville. Now a corporal, Wolpe was a somewhat eccentric Jewish guy who had graduated from Newberg Free Academy High School in New York. The Lieutenant remembered from their enlisted days in Jacksonville that Jack had been too embarrassed to cash his meager PFC paycheck of twenty dollars every two weeks because he had family money. To Jack, a draftee, the twenty dollars amounted to chump change. Instead, he neatly stacked each and every one of those paychecks in his wall locker, uncashed.

In the States, Wolpe drove a brand new, maroon-colored 1965 Chevy Impala. Later, he traded that car for a shiny white Corvette. He used to race the 'Vette on the local drag strip near the Naval Air Station. At that time, a group of guys, including the Lieutenant, frequented the drag strip on Saturday nights to cheer Wolpe on. It was one of only a few worthwhile, cheap entertainments the men from the barracks enjoyed.

Jack Wolpe passed the word on that he had bumped into the Lieutenant to Corporal Jack Gottlieb and PFC Hicks, men who were also part of the Jacksonville gang in 1965. All three men found themselves as members of the Third Recon Battalion operating out of Phu Bai.

In Jacksonville, Jack Gottlieb, a serious man, earned the title of "Most Gung Ho Marine" in the barracks. He dressed impeccably.

His combat boots were always spit-shined and his brass belt buckle smartly polished. His uniform stayed squared away; shirt starched and perfectly creased, with no hanging threads in view. Gottlieb always looked like the recruiting poster Marine.

PFC Hicks arrived at Marine Barracks in Jacksonville in May, 1965, eight months after the Lieutenant had arrived. It was Hicks' first duty station following boot camp. PFC Hicks was serious minded and attentive to his duties. He hailed from upstate New York, and he sometimes joined with Wolpe, Gottlieb, and the Lieutenant (then a lance corporal) when they had liberty.

Soon afterwards, the Lieutenant saw the three old pals together and told them about Sergeant Amos' death. They reacted with dismay. By then, a number of men from the old barracks days had been killed. Sergeant Amos' death was another sad casualty in a war that had already taken too many young men's lives. The four men spoke for about ten minutes. They talked mostly about their recon missions in the A Shau Valley. This was the same valley where the big US 175mm artillery was firing as a part of Operation Cumberland.

About a week later, while passing thru Phu Bai again, the Lieutenant ran into PFC Hicks, who gave him the news that Jack Wolpe, the racing car enthusiast, had just been killed on a mission near the A Shau Valley. It happened when a helicopter had come in to extract Wolpe's team from their location. After the men boarded the chopper, it took a direct hit from an NVA RPG rocket. The chopper simultaneously exploded and rolled down a hill, killing everyone on board. The Lieutenant was beginning to lose track of the number of men from the Jacksonville Marine Barracks who had been killed. It was becoming harder and harder to push his emotions down while going forward with his duties.

CHAPTER 13

ENTERTAINMENT

AUGUST AND SEPTEMBER 1967

West of Phu Bai and Hue City, Operation Cumberland, the continuing combat operation, ran from mid-June until August 17. Cumberland was an operation in which Marine companies or battalions were continually rotated in and out at a point east of the A Shau Valley every few weeks. When the operation finally ended, Alpha Company, who had participated in the operation, moved to a rock-crushing site along the road to Phu Bai. Their mission was to provide security for the engineers. The Marines of Alpha Company patrolled the surrounding areas on a twenty-four-hour basis.

All day, enormous, heavy-rock crushing machines turned boulders into gravel. The machines had been trucked up from Phu Bai and were a part of the massive amount of equipment brought in-country from the US. The boulders came from the nearby hills. The machines worked tirelessly to pulverize the brownish rocks and spit them out, like a mechanical giant spewing rotten ground meat from its mouth. Using the crushed rock, the engineers "paved" the road during the day. The ultimate purpose of crushing the rocks was to use the gravel to help strengthen and stabilize the dirt road leading from Phu Bai to the A Shau Valley.

At the rock-crushing site, the engineers built jungle huts to house themselves as well as Alpha Company. Each structure consisted of a wooden floor with plywood siding four feet high on all four sides and screens above the plywood. The huts were topped with tin roofs. They were large enough to hold nearly ten men, and were a big improvement from the foxhole and bunker living of the previous few months. For a change, the men of A Company slept on cots instead of hard-packed dirt.

Using portable generators, the engineers also provided electricity to the huts—a novelty in such a remote location. Electricity was a big deal. Having electricity meant not only light by which to see at night, but it also made nighttime entertainment possible. The Lieutenant managed to procure a small black and white TV from special services at Camp Evans. Unfortunately, the only shows broadcast were reruns of a 1950's series depicting action during WWII, called *Combat*.

The irony wasn't lost on anyone. Each evening, about twenty or twenty-five men would gather around the small TV set. They booed, scoffed, swore, and laughed at the goofy TV portrayal of combat, because they knew firsthand the harsh realities of the real deal of battle.

Later, the Lieutenant, in a conversation with his company commander, Captain Keith Thompson, discussed how ridiculous the TV series was. In the show, the company commander didn't engage with his troops, but instead remained far removed from their day-to-day lives.

"Yep," Thompson agreed. "That TV commander was probably sitting back in a hut somewhere listening to a radio or watching movies just like we are right now with this here TV. It's sure not reality. Those officers in the story are not out there with their troops like we are. They look like mamma's boys," he continued.

Both men chuckled. They were entertained by the troops' lively reaction to the show. It felt good to laugh at the men's often outrageously funny comments.

The television the troops watched in the hut was a far cry from the live USO shows starring Bob Hope and beautiful starlets and actresses from Hollywood who came over to Vietnam to entertain the troops. Those shows were taped, then later televised as "Christmas Specials" to portray the troops overseas being entertained during their "spare time" as a kind of "diversion" from war. Whatever diversions the shows provided, and however well-meaning they were, no one anywhere near the northern I Corps/DMZ area had ever seen that kind of live entertainment! Absolutely no one! The only troops privileged to attend such an extravaganza were the guys back in the safety of the rear, somewhere around the Da Nang area.

RELIGIOUS SERVICES

Another more practical diversion for the men was the religious services. These services were sporadic and could be either Catholic or Protestant. The Lieutenant attended any religious service whenever he could, which was seldom. He wasn't picky, though. The Catholic Mass was familiar, as the Lieutenant had been raised Catholic. However, the Protestant services were a good mix of Bible reading with preaching.

At Camp Evans, a replacement Catholic priest had recently been assigned to the Fourth Marine Regiment. He periodically said Mass for whoever happened to be present at the time. The day of the week was unimportant. Unfortunately, the Catholic services were only sparsely attended because the priest mumbled the Mass prayers, leaving the attendees feeling flat. His sermons didn't provide much inspiration for the men, either. Additionally, the new

Catholic chaplain seemed unwilling to visit the troops in the field. He tended to concentrate on shuffling Red Cross messages, something not unnoticed by the men.

The Catholic "padre," as all military chaplains were called, was contrasted and compared by the men to Father Steve Almasy, the new chaplain's predecessor. Father Almasy was someone whom the men trusted and respected. At Phu Bai, Almasy had said Mass on a makeshift altar of ammo boxes stacked high. He regularly and fearlessly visited the troops in the field. Even when under intense gunfire, he administered last rites to dying Marines and brought comfort to the wounded. Unfortunately for Father Steve, he was never decorated for his bravery in action, simply because his battalion commander, who authorized awards, didn't like Catholics.

After attending a Protestant service in August at Camp Evans, the Lieutenant had an epiphany. He decided that Protestants had a higher view of a relationship with God, and they seemed more sincere about their beliefs. He felt men must respect one another as Christians, and not just because of a particular denomination. He began to view the beliefs a man held in his heart as more important than denominational affiliation. Additionally, the Lieutenant looked forward to the Protestant Bible readings and the sermons more than he did the Mass.

LET ME COUNT THE WAYS

Despite the Lieutenant's new and sometimes profound thoughts about God and religious denominations, he still struggled with thoughts of impending doom. Lying on his cot, unable to sleep, the Lieutenant ticked off to himself a list of possible endings that could be anyone's undoing, including anti-personnel mines, grenades, punji pits, gunshots, direct or indirect artillery or mortar fire, shrapnel, flame throwers, helicopter crashes, or amtrac explosions, and also by sniper fire, friendly fire, bombs, even Jeep or truck accidents. There might be even more ways he hadn't remembered! Just a variety of "opportunities" for the skulking Dark Demon to sneak up, grab someone, and take them away.

I don't want to die here. I want to go home. I want to go home under my own steam, not maimed, and not in a flag-draped coffin.

Still unable to sleep, the Lieutenant turned his thoughts once more toward his wife. He tried to picture her face, but that was becoming more difficult. He was glad for the picture of her he always carried with him. He enjoyed looking at it. He remembered so many little things about her, though, like the night they were on a date when they were still teenagers. She was sitting next to him in the car as he drove her home, and he remembered the exact moment when he stole a sideways glance at her and thought to himself, *I could spend the rest of my life with her.* It was that moment when he knew he wanted ed to marry her. Sometimes, the Lieutenant thought the only thing keeping him sane was the moments when he remembered his wife.

SEPTEMBER 21-25, 1967
R&R

Somewhere nearly halfway across the Pacific on the flight to Hawaii, the Lieutenant's 707 jet plane landed on a small island airstrip. There, the planeload of anxious men on their way to a much needed R&R sat—and sat. No explanation was given, and the men remained sweating in their seats on the runway for more than five torturous hours, anticipating Hawaii and their loved ones.

Lieutenant Biff Mullins was the Lieutenant's seatmate. They had been in The Basic School together the previous year. They chatted some, but mostly they tried to nap. Mullins asked the Lieutenant about his R&R plans.

"My wife and I are just staying put in Honolulu," the Lieutenant replied. "What about you?"

"My wife and I are flying over to Maui once we get to Honolulu. She has planned a second honeymoon for us in a resort hotel there. I can't wait. I just want to be out of Asia, and forget about the war, if only for a few days." Biff said.

"Maui is more secluded than Honolulu, and we just want peace and quiet. We don't want to be around any rowdiness from other servicemen," Biff continued.

The Lieutenant agreed that Biff had a good plan. They both went back to daydreaming about the upcoming reunion with their wives.

Later, they chatted some about the war, in which part of Vietnam they were currently serving, their units, and others they had seen or heard about from their Basic School class. But, like everyone else, they wanted to arrive in Hawaii ASAP. The date was September 21, and the Lieutenant hadn't seen his wife in more than nine long months. He was also a father who had never seen his son. He knew this could be his final meeting with his wife. He wanted every second they had together to count.

When the plane finally landed, the men walked through the processing area that was separated from the general arrival area by a tall glass divider. He could see women on the other side, and he strained his eyes to pick out his wife's face from among the many females. American women—blondes, brunettes, dark haired, and a few redheads—all stood waiting. At the sight of the men, a stampede ensued. A crush of women one side pressed closer into the glass and scanned the crowd to spot a familiar face. A rush of men did the same on the opposite side of the arrival window. Squeals of shear joy erupted as women glimpsed their men. On the women's side, the Lieutenant's wife had no trouble identifying him in the crowd of shorthaired warriors, and she told him so later. She said she recognized his height, head, and bearing instantly. He didn't see her at first, but when he finally located her, he grinned and motioned her to the exit where they'd meet, skipping the moments at the glass divider altogether. The exit was clogged with a line-up of men squeezing through the passageway to embrace their loved ones. Those behind them had to wait for others to get out of the way. Everyone was impatient.

The Lieutenant dropped his duffle bag and swept his wife off her feet, giving her a bear hug. She was only a slip of a girl. She felt like she'd break in his arms, but he couldn't stop hugging her. They didn't release their embrace for some minutes. But they weren't free to go just yet. There was still the formality of the mandatory military briefing.

Happy couples, along with a few infants, were bussed to the Army's Fort DeRussy, a few miles away, for the required briefing. No one paid any attention to the instructions, though. The excitement was too great. Some of the couples left immediately afterwards for another island, but most opted to stay on Oahu. Honolulu held plenty of entertainment and was just more convenient. Besides, no further travel time was required. Those going to an outlying island, like Maui or the big island of Hawaii, had another plane to catch.

The Lieutenant's wife had already booked a hotel for them near Waikiki Beach through a travel agent. However, when she'd arrived the evening before, she'd found the room completely unsatisfactory. The accommodations had twin beds. The "ocean view" advertised in the travel brochure turned out to be non-existent unless you went to the roof. The room itself was small, musty, and damp. By that time, though, she was just too exhausted from traveling to switch hotels. The next morning, her efforts were spent getting to the airport to await the Lieutenant's arrival. She did manage, however, to find out the name of a much better hotel.

So their first order of business was to move out of the dingy hotel and into the new high-rise Ilikai, a highly recommended, top-rated vacation spot on Honolulu's Waikiki Beach. During the transfer of their bags, she was so distracted that she dropped a very expensive bottle of champagne, a gift from their best man, Chuck. She'd brought it all the way from the East Coast in her carry-on only to see it shattered and bubbling on the pavement. The Lieutenant thought it was like the shattered and broken bodies bleeding out in the dirt. He didn't believe in omens, but the image gave him pause.

For a few days, the Lieutenant and his wife basked in each other's company. Being together seemed surreal. Hawaii truly was a beautiful, tropical paradise. Colorful flowers of all varieties bloomed everywhere. The climate was warm and sunny, and the atmosphere laidback. The Lieutenant tried to relax but found himself repeatedly looking over his shoulder. He was still in combat mode.

They drove around the island in their rented car and stopped to eat fresh pineapple from the field. A local showed them how to salt the pineapple to bring out its juicy flavor. They checked out spectacular ocean views from Diamond Head. They took pictures. Then they visited the USS *Arizona* War Memorial, a sober reminder of the horrors of World War II, roughly twenty-six years before, when the Japanese bombed Pearl Harbor. They wished they'd skipped that landmark destination. It was awe inspiring, but hit a little too close to home.

Later that night, the Lieutenant startled his wife out of her sleep when he awoke to find himself sweating and on the floor yelling, "106! 106! 106!"

In his dream, he was trying to roll into a foxhole to escape from enemy 106mm recoilless rifle fire. A few 106s had been captured by the NVA early in the Vietnam War. The NVA used the 106s to fire back at the Marines. This weapon gave no early warning sound of being fired. The 106s rounds flew in a direct line like a bullet. The impact hit in less than a second or two. It was not a weapon the Marines wanted in the NVA's hands, yet in the battle of Con Thien, the enemy regularly peppered the defensive line with fire from this weapon.

His wife came to the floor next to him. She wrapped her arms around him and tried to assure him that it was just a bad dream. She encouraged him to come back to bed, but he didn't right away. He needed a few drinks to settle his nerves. When his wife went back to bed, he sat in a cushy armchair in the corner of the room watching her sleep. He envied the fact that she could return to sleep so quickly. He longed for the time when he could relax enough to believe that there were no life-threatening dangers lurking about. Noise from outside the hotel could have triggered the Lieutenant's reaction. He felt out of control, and wondered if he would have similar vivid dreams in the future. He'd heard of men having these types of violent wartime dreams, but never imagined he'd suffer from them. The incident caused the Lieutenant to become uneasy about himself. His self-confidence was badly shaken by the dream.

THE DON HO SHOW

The Don Ho show was a Hawaiian must. Everyone who'd come back from R&R said so. The Lieutenant and his wife saw the show on their last evening of R&R. Nightly, this lively entertainment catered to the servicemen on R&R who took a brief respite from the war. This show featured dancing hula girls on stage, girls who apparently had a knack for spotting the shyest of the servicemen. On the evening the Lieutenant and his wife attended the outdoor show, one pretty, grass-skirted hula girl walked down from the stage into the audience. Almost immediately, she spotted the Lieutenant, took him by the hand, and led him back on stage to dance with her. Bringing men on stage made the evening more entertaining. The servicemen the girls chose often stammered and blushed their way through the experience, thoroughly embarrassed. The Lieutenant was no exception. He didn't like a fuss made over him, and he couldn't dance. He just wanted to get back to his seat.

The showgirls crowned their raven hair with halos of flowers—hair that grew straight and long and hung down to their waists. Dressed in native costumes of bra-like tops and grass skirts with leis around their necks and anklets of flowers on their bare feet, they shook up the stage to the beat of the Hawaiian drummers nearby. The beautiful girls made the men's eyes pop.

The Don Ho Show also included men twirling fire batons. They dressed in native costumes. They wore dark-colored shorts but were barefooted and shirtless. They also wore green leaf necklaces, and leaf crowns on their heads, like laurel wreaths. They spun the fire batons around with amazing dexterity. They wowed the audience when they threw the fire sticks up into the air and caught them again. A luau with roasted pig and various buffet side dishes were all included in the admission price. Pina coladas arrived from the bar with tiny umbrellas atop the drinks. The mood was festive, and the audience joined in singing "Tiny Bubbles," accompanied by men playing ukuleles. Everyone, it seemed, knew the words: "Tiny bubbles/in the wine/make me feel happy/make me feel fine. Tiny bubbles/make me warm all over/with a feelin' that I'm gonna love you/'til the end of time."

As the song continued, everyone went native, enjoying something touristy, tropical, and fun. For at least a short while, couples and the few single men could forget about the war. Having his wife by his side in the exotic setting with romantic, warm night breezes under swaying palm trees seemed to help sooth the Lieutenant, at least temporarily.

What spoiled their Hawaiian experience was the dread that still hung over all the couples—knowing they only had those few precious days together before having to tear themselves away from one another yet again.

When the evening was over, and when the R&R time finished, their grief hung heavy, yet unspoken between them. Early the next morning, as the Lieutenant's plane prepared to taxi for take off, he managed to find his wife in the crowd of women, bravely waving her tearful good byes. He knew she couldn't see him at the airplane window, but like every man returning to war, he couldn't help but wonder *Will this be our last memory of each other?*

SEPTEMBER 26, 1967
POST R&R

At Camp Evans, after one day back in Vietnam, Hawaii already seemed like a distant dream; the Lieutenant could hardly believe Hawaii happened at all. He had been transported to another world, but now he was back to drudgery. For a few glorious days, he'd been alone with his wife, feeling elated like a schoolboy, but again he had to face his own dismal reality of being a Marine at war.

Nowhere near long enough, he told himself. *How is it possible to miss one person so much? She's always on my mind, even though we're a half a world apart. No wonder guys lose their focus when they return from R&R.*

In late September, the Lieutenant moved to Quang Tri to be with Alpha and Bravo Companies, who were providing security during the building of an airstrip. The existing airstrip farther north at Dong Ha had become too dangerous because of NVA rockets, therefore making it unsafe for take offs and landings. The new airstrip was located out of the range of both NVA rockets and artillery.

Just as he had feared, the Lieutenant *did* let his guard down after his return from Hawaii. He was walking the Quang Tri perimeter, checking his company's defensive position, when a mortar barrage started. His immediate instinct was to lie flat. But the Lieutenant hadn't realized he had walked far too close to the scout Marine K-9s chained up nearby. He didn't have time to hit the deck before a growling German shepherd bit into his leg right where he stood. The dog planted its fierce fangs firmly into the Lieutenant's right calf just above his boot. Its big teeth ripped through the Lieutenant's utility trousers. It felt like the bite went all the way into his bone. The Lieutenant stood stark still, swearing at the dog, while cursing himself for his carelessness.

Fortunately, the handler happened to be nearby and saw what had happened. As soon as the incoming exploded, he called out to the Lieutenant,

"Hold as still as possible! Don't move."

The Lieutenant had no intention of moving—not while the dog still had him trapped by the leg. The handler quickly called the dog off, explaining that the dog must have been spooked by the explosion noise. The shepherd immediately obeyed, but by then the damage was done. The handler never expressed any remorse for the dog's behavior. He didn't apologize. The puncture wounds from the dog bite hurt like hell and needed immediate attention. At the Quang Tri med station, the doc fixed up the Lieutenant. He limped around for a couple of weeks until he eventually healed.

The dog bite, however, was enough to serve as a wake-up call for the Lieutenant. He still had four months left in-country before his tour of duty would be over.

Quit daydreaming and pay attention to the work at hand, he reminded himself. *Keep your focus, man, or you'll be dead soon.*

The final phase of his thirteen-month tour was not easy. The Lieutenant was bored. He wished he could either be in the thick of things fighting alongside his men, or back with his wife in the utopia of the Hawaiian Islands. To him, the trouble with war was that he vacillated between terror, boredom, and longing—just like the old saying "War is monotonously tedious, punctuated by unexpected and surprising moments of terror."

BIFF'S FATE

Only a few days later on the thirtieth, the Lieutenant received word that Lieutenant Biff Mullins, who had been his seatmate on the flight over and back from Hawaii, had been killed at the DMZ. He had been with the Second Battalion, Fourth Marines. They had the same control date for rotation home.

Biff must have lost his focus, the Lieutenant reckoned. *That's what happens when you get distracted by R&R. It's too damn hard coming back. For a while, you think you just might make it outta here alive, and then another buddy gets it. Nothing's a sure thing. What's the point of making friends, or even getting a little bit attached to people? They just die. They all die. Every day there's more death. I don't want to even talk to people anymore. It doesn't seem worth the effort.*

The news of Biff Mullins' death changed something inside the Lieutenant. It marked the beginning of his slide into a thick, black cloud of depression. He wrote home less often because he couldn't think of anything to say. He avoided social conversations because they took too much energy. Sleeplessness plagued him. Like the gathering storm clouds of the rainy season now upon them, an eerie darkness had been steadily creeping up on him for months. He was at a loss to stop either.

CHAPTER 14

OPERATIONS OFFICER ASSISTANT (S-3A)

OCTOBER AND NOVEMBER 1967

On October 3, the Lieutenant gained another new assignment. This time he would become the S-3A, the battalion assistant operations officer for the First Battalion, Fourth Marines located at Camp Evans. This was the base camp for the entire Fourth Marine Regiment.

The camp was located north of Phu Bai and south of Dong Ha. The Lieutenant was assigned to the Battalion Combat Operations Center to write reports and other boring administrative duties.

The Lieutenant's new responsibilities included reading all incoming and outgoing radio messages, and taking appropriate action. For example, if Bravo Company requested a resupply of ammunition, the message would be rerouted to the S-4 (logistics) for action. The request was sent either by radio or hand carried. Another example: an intelligence report from the regimental S-2 (intelligence) to the First Battalion. It would be disseminated to the commanding officer, executive officer, and S-3, and the appropriate company commander for action and for information. In other words, the Lieutenant supervised all messages received, sent, and disseminated. This operation went on twenty-four hours a day, seven days a week. Work shifts were twelve hours on, and twelve hours off, divided between five officers.

The radio operators recorded the messages in writing. The messages were kept in sequential order for the command chronology. The chronology was a monthly recording of historical and operational events of the battalion. Additionally, the Lieutenant was charged with drafting this end-of-the-month report for the major's approval. Once approved, the report was submitted to the regiment. Someone at regimental headquarters forwarded the reports to the Third Marine Division, and eventually to Headquarters Marine Corps in Washington, DC, to be reviewed and archived with other historical records.

Additionally, the Lieutenant had full charge of all enlisted personnel, six men, in the operations center. He set up the schedule for the various staff officers to be the watch commanders. They would be in the Combat Operations Center on alert to respond to action messages when received. Sometimes the Lieutenant delivered messages by Jeep or truck, or occasionally by helicopter, to Dong Ha or Phu Bai.

It was during this time as S-3A that the Lieutenant discovered that some of the command chronologies were inaccurate and contained errors. He particularly noted that the number of casualties reported on incoming radio messages was often wrong. He knew this because he had participated in some of the very actions that were being reported. These radio messages were the basis of facts about battles and enemy actions. The radio operators, on both the transmitting and receiving end, did not accurately record some of these messages. It was just human error. The subsequent chain of reporting created more errors. Unfortunately, these errors and inaccuracies were passed up the chain of command. This would include the situation reports, after-action reports, and the command chronologies. The command chronologies were critical because they would be the base document from which the history of the Vietnam Conflict would ultimately be recorded for posterity and archived in historical vaults.

When the Lieutenant brought the situation about the inaccurate reporting to his superior, Major Hal Nelson, the battalion S-3, he verified the Lieutenant's findings, but little could be done to correct previous reporting. Nelson then put into place a verification review on all messages to insure present and future messages were factually correct.

The Lieutenant's "office" was only a general-purpose tent with field radios on rickety tables, along with a few wooden field desks and benches. There was, however, one advantage. He was able to stay in touch with the day-to-day operations of each company and their commanders at both the company and platoon levels. Meanwhile, Alpha Company remained nearby at Camp Evans providing perimeter security. Being the S-3A was a captain's job, and a much better assignment than most others he could have been given, yet the Lieutenant still itched to be with his men where the action was.

LEGAL DEALINGS

Occasionally, the Lieutenant would be tagged to serve as trial or defense counsel for someone being court-martialed. In one example, a private first class got tired of war, shot himself in the foot, and claimed it was an accident. Initially, the man was medivaced. Later, after he'd recovered, the man was returned to duty. But the battalion commander put him on report and chose to court-martial him so he would be an example to deter others from attempting the same. The private was charged with dereliction of duty by a self-inflicted wound to avoid combat. When his case went to trial, the Lieutenant was appointed as his defense counsel.

The prosecuting officer, a captain, failed to prove his case because he didn't have any witnesses to the actual shooting. So, the Lieutenant won the case for the private first class. Of course, everyone knew the guy really had shot himself in the foot, and the Lieutenant was quite pissed off that he won, because he knew the private was guilty as hell.

Another time, the Lieutenant served as a defense counsel for a corporal accused of unauthorized absence (UA). The man was on a three-day R&R in the Philippines and stayed over two extra days. He was picked up by the shore patrol (Navy military police) and was returned to his battalion in Vietnam. It was a special court-martial, and the three officers who sat in judgment found the man guilty. But the Lieutenant pleaded the corporal's case, saying that the man had extenuating family circumstances. The corporal was distraught by his mother's illness, and for some unknown reason, couldn't communicate with her. He had been trying to reach her by phone. He'd been in the battalion, enduring almost ten months of combat, with only two months left on his tour. Instead of stripping the man of his rank (reducing his rank to private), he was fined only fifty dollars by the president of the court, one of the three sitting officers. The corporal wasn't a bad man. The Lieutenant felt this was a win.

MESS TENT DINING

Since his arrival at Camp Evans, the Lieutenant ate in the mess tent daily. The chow was dished out on metal trays by the cooks, usually privates, who slopped it into the tray's small compartments. Most of it tasted like cardboard. The burnt meat was barely chewable; instant mashed potatoes, chalk-like. Food was rarely served hot. On the few occasions when vegetables showed up, they were served ice cold. Eating salad greens covered in grit from the daily dust storms proved challenging. The coffee tasted like mud. The Lieutenant had to remind himself to be thankful that he wasn't eating C-rations, so he tried to make the best of it. Besides, he wasn't one to complain. At least not out loud. *I need to be grateful that I'm alive and able to eat,* he reminded himself.

After one particularly bad dining experience, he sat alone on a wooden dining hall bench, smoking and staring into his half-empty coffee cup. He remembered early in their marriage when his new bride had chosen to surprise him with one of the few dishes in her cooking repertoire she felt confident enough to make—creamed chipped beef. The Lieutenant had a deadly aversion to creamed chipped beef. The stuff caused him to vomit whenever he ate it. But out of respect for his wife's culinary efforts, he had gagged it down wordlessly at dinner and had promptly gotten sick about an hour later. Then he quietly asked her not to make that particular dish again because it had sickened him. Shocked by his revelation, she vowed never to cook creamed chipped beef again.

Another time in one of his wife's early attempts to wow him with her baking skills, she baked her first apple pie from scratch. He sighed, remembering the sweet aroma of apples and cinnamon wafting through the air as she pulled the pie from the oven. His mouth watered as he saw the crust had cooked to a perfect brown. All was well, until he tasted the pie and realized she'd somehow forgotten to add any sugar.

I love her, but I sure hope her cooking has improved since I've been away. Well, at least her fried chicken is good, he mused.

OCTOBER 23, 1967
SURPRISE FROM HOME

As S-3A, the Lieutenant was responsible for making rounds between Camp Evans, Phu Bai, and Quang Tri regularly. Two companies, A and C, were at Quang Tri. On October 23, he stopped at Quang Tri to write up a few operation reports. He wasn't inside a general-purpose tent. Instead, he was crouched under his poncho that he used as shelter-half to keep the rain off. He just wanted a little quiet. This late in October the monsoon rains were in full swing. Day after day, it continually rained, with only short periods of let-up. This meant mud everywhere. The dampness made his jaw throb. He knew he'd be glad when he could get the shrapnel removed from his face and hoped it wouldn't hurt as much then. He rubbed his jaw as he sat alone on an old ammo box. Someone delivering US mail found him and brought a batch of letters. He was curious when he saw the nine-by-twelve-inch brown manila envelope addressed to him in his wife's handwriting.

When he tore the envelope open, leaves came tumbling out—leaves of every variety, color, and description: chestnut brown, and russet-red oak leaves, crimson maple leaves, yellow, moss green walnut and elm leaves. Some were multicolored in their own right. Amber, golden, and scarlet—a mixed variety of shapes and sizes fell into his lap. Autumn at home! What a gift! Even the dry smell of them made him nearly delirious with homesickness. Hurriedly, he gathered them up and stuffed them back into the envelope so not one would be lost, get wet, or become ruined.

His wife knew that autumn was always his favorite season. This was her way of sending him a little piece of home. He closed his eyes and inhaled the earthy scent from the envelope once again. It seemed like a decadent, forbidden luxury. He remembered nostalgically their magical day trip to the Skyline Parkway a year ago, when they'd enjoyed scenic views and picnicked at their leisure.

"Thank you, honey," he whispered.

As soon as he returned to his tent, he tucked the surprise foliage inside his waterproof bag for safekeeping. Over the next few weeks, he often pulled out the envelope to relish its contents and think of home.

NOVEMBER 1967
OPERATION GRANITE

By the end of October, security duty for the airstrip at Quang Tri for the First Battalion, Fourth Marines finished. The entire battalion moved back to Camp Evans to prepare for another operation. This one was named Operation Granite.

NOVEMBER 4, 1967
PACKAGE FROM PENNSYLVANIA

In early November, a package arrived from Sergeant Jack Gottlieb, formerly Corporal Gottlieb. He had returned safely home in Pennsylvania after his combat duty had finished. Now a civilian, Jack was the "best dressed," squared-away Marine from the Jacksonville enlisted men who the Lieutenant had bumped into at Phu Bai, back in July.

The package contained a small King James Bible. A short note accompanied the Bible saying that he hoped the Lieutenant would take comfort from reading its passages. The Bible was small enough to fit in the Lieutenant's side trouser pocket, so he put it there in the plastic bag where he kept the pictures of his wife and son. It made his pocket bulge some, but he was accustomed to that. From time to time, he read it if he had nothing else to do. He read Genesis, then skipped over to the New Testament, where he was a little more familiar with some of the stories. He'd heard portions of the Gospels and Epistles during Mass since childhood, but had practically no knowledge of the Old Testament.

What a considerate gift. Jack always was a decent sort. He's a good Protestant. I wonder what prompted him to send this. Well, it's a good thing to have, and I appreciate it.

The Lieutenant wrote a thank-you note to Jack to let him know he found the gift thoughtful.

JOINT OPERATION

During the first weeks of November, the Fourth Marines launched a joint operation with the First Army of the Republic of Vietnam (ARVN) Division to clear out the NVA operating bases in the mountains to the west of the Co Bi Than Tan Valley. The First Battalion, Fourth Marines, led by Company A, would attack the hills and mountains from the north. The Lieutenant was assigned as the liaison to a regiment of the First ARVN Division, which was to attack the mountains from the south side.

The Lieutenant and a Marine radio operator, a corporal from Headquarters and Service Company, were driven by Jeep to the ARVN headquarters, just north of Hue City. The ARVN compound consisted of a series of much more upscale jungle huts than existed at Camp Evans. There, the Lieutenant met up with Captain J. J. Cooligan, United States Marine Corps, who had been one of the Lieutenant's instructors at The Basic School in Quantico the previous year. Cooligan didn't remember the Lieutenant because he was only one of over a thousand lieutenants who'd passed through training that year. Cooligan taught

Explosives and Demolition at The Basic School. He was a tall, lanky man, about six five, and skinny as a beanpole. The most memorable thing about him, though, was his completely calm demeanor. He never seemed to become rattled, an admirable and appropriate trait for someone handling explosive materials.

"Good to see you, Captain. I remember you, especially because of your demolition and weapons classes."

"Yeah, that sure seems like a very long time ago now," Cooligan replied with a sideways grin.

"How long have you been here, sir?"

"About six months."

Looking around at the Captain's quarters, the Lieutenant couldn't help but compare them to the accommodations in which he and his men had been living—open foxholes versus the "luxury" living the Captain enjoyed. Even contrasted to his tent and cot at Camp Evans, the Captain's lodgings seemed almost like the Ritz. In his headquarters with the ARVN, Captain Cooligan was billeted in a long, low, wooden building with a tin roof. The building was equipped with most of the modern conveniences; amenities only fondly remembered by just about every combatant of Alpha Company since first entering Vietnam. For starters, the entire building was air-conditioned. It also boasted electricity and running water, with indoor bathrooms and showers down the hall. The Captain's room doubled as his office. His cot sat in the corner. He had privacy. It was difficult not to be envious.

"Looks like you've got some fairly comfortable living quarters here, sir."

"Yeah, but it's only by appearances. It's really not that great here," Cooligan replied dryly.

The Lieutenant figured out by the Captain's response that this was code for how difficult it was working with the ARVN, and how differently they thought and did things from the Marines. Cooligan, being a US advisor, had no command or decision-making authority. He was there in a purely advisory capacity, something extremely difficult for any Marine at war.

The Lieutenant teamed up with Captain Cooligan and his radioman and joined the regimental advisor, a US Army major, who was the senior advisor for the ARVN Regiment. The entire regiment, plus the few US advisors, the Lieutenant, and his radioman were then flown by helicopter from their compound near Hue to the south side of the mountains overlooking the Co Bi Than Tan Valley.

Once the regiment landed, the ARVN began attacking the enemy on the south side of the mountains. The terrain was extremely difficult: steep, rocky, with a heavy tree canopy and a narrow ridgeline on top. Everyone had no choice but to move single file. There were sporadic attacks, but no heavy enemy contact was encountered. The Lieutenant stayed in radio contact with the S-3 of First Battalion, Fourth Marines to coordinate the movements and artillery fire support during the operation.

It wasn't long before the Lieutenant got Cooligan's drift about things being good there, but only by appearances. After a few days, drinking water ran out for the ARVN troops. The men required an emergency supply of water to be airlifted in, but the helicopters couldn't land at the location due to the extensive tree canopies. The men in the ARVN choppers began dropping canisters of water down to the troops from an altitude of about thirty feet. The metal canisters, which held about five gallons of water each, had once been used for artillery gunpowder. These normally would be good containers to hold water because they were airtight but dropping them from such a height caused many canisters to break apart. Everyone was so thirsty, a mad scramble ensued for any canisters that still contained water. ARVN troops were grabbing the canisters without regard to any organized process. Four or five men fought over one canister. Once a man had a canister firmly in his hands, he opened the lid and guzzled water without sharing. When a man drank his fill, he dropped the canister, spilling water on the ground with no thought to conserving what remained. The ARVN officers participated in the scramble for water as well. Captain Cooligan had seen it all before, so he stayed out of the fray. The Lieutenant looked on in disbelief. It looked like the ARVN discipline had completely broken down. The men's thirst was greater than the supply of water, and the result was the survival of the fittest. Fortunately for the Lieutenant, his radioman managed to get one of the containers for himself, the Lieutenant, and Captain Cooligan to share.

The Marines, by comparison, had much better supply connections, and would never have waited until they were completely out of water to call in by radio for resupplies. Nor would their discipline have broken down during the distribution of food or water. The Marines had a structured method of supply distribution in place. It was orderly and it worked.

During Operation Granite, the ARVN only encountered light resistance from the NVA. No heavy causalities were reported. The NVA were driven out of the mountains in about four days of intense fighting on the north side. From the Lieutenant's point of view, this operation with the ARVN was a cakewalk. However, on the north side of the mountain with the First Battalion, Fourth Marines, the NVA resistance was intense.

The Lieutenant felt more despondent than ever after Operation Granite because he realized yet again that the ARVN were not ready to take on their enemy, the North Vietnamese. And this operation was costing American lives. The Lieutenant believed joint operations like these were strictly for political show. Once again, he blamed the politicians in Washington, as well as the news media, for the mess they had made.

Alpha Company suffered a number killed and many wounded. One of those killed was Corporal Robert Agar, who had previously been one of the Lieutenant's machine gunners. The Lieutenant responded to the news of yet another killed in action of someone he knew with a mix of anger, frustration, and sadness. Agar had been a good guy, and he was near the end of his tour. Hailing from West Virginia, Agar had taken his job seriously, and he was well esteemed by his fellow platoon members. He took his Christianity seriously, too, and seemed reverent towards God in a compelling way.

The Lieutenant moaned inwardly, *Why are we digging our own grave in this country? There seems to be no way out. We can't possibly win this war. It won't end well for anyone except the NVA.*

At the end of Operation Granite, the Lieutenant had to maneuver along with a few US advisors off the mountaintop by foot to get to where the tree canopy diminished enough for him to be picked up by helicopter. As he headed toward the valley, he was amazed to see an enormous concrete statue of the Blessed Virgin Mary with her arms outstretched over the Co Bi Than Tan Valley, as if to render divine protection. The Lieutenant wondered how they'd maneuvered the statue up there, given the rugged terrain. He knew no helicopter could have brought it there. He surmised the statue must have been cast in concrete and assembled where it stood.

As the helicopter lifted him up over the canopy and the statue, the Lieutenant thought, *she sure blew her job of protecting the many thousands who have been killed in this valley since the war began. To think that a statue could provide any protection seems an odd thing for Vietnamese Catholics to believe, anyhow.*

For the Lieutenant, his part in Operation Granite ended with him being transported by a US Army (Huey) UH1E helicopter gunship back to Camp Evans. All the Lieutenant could think was *This has been one more wasted and ill-conceived operation trying to demonstrate the value of ARVN and US forces working together. The ARVN just aren't ready to take on the North Vietnamese.*

On November 27, the battalion, along with the Lieutenant, moved from Camp Evans to Dong Ha. The different operations often overlapped, and battalions or companies were sometimes shifted from one operation to another with little notice. He went to Dong Ha to participate in Operation Buffalo. Operation Buffalo ran concurrently with Operation Kentucky, using men from First Battalion, Fourth Marine Regiment to reinforce the Ninth Marine Regiment. The Lieutenant went back to the monotony of admin duty.

CHAPTER 15

OP CENTER CHANGES

DECEMBER 2, 1967

Operation Kentucky began on December 2. The Lieutenant continued to work in the Operations Center receiving and disseminating messages. Realizing these reports were giving details about some of the men he'd commanded earlier in the year, he could see that Alpha Company was right back at the DMZ where they had been last May, and with little change.

Life at the DMZ continued to be deadly. In addition, the weather had turned cold, wet, and miserable, fanned by high winds. The Lieutenant felt sorry that the men suffered out in the open with no relief from wind, rain, or cold. Because of low visibility, there was no air-to-ground support for the troops at the DMZ. This meant no advantage for air power to drop bombs on North Vietnamese forces. Another disadvantage was that helicopter gunships were rendered useless. They couldn't fly in the heavy monsoon rains and low cloud cover. Besides, the gunships were too slow. They could be easily shot down by the NVA's anti-aircraft .50-caliber machine guns.

By this time, the Lieutenant could see that morale was at an all-time low, not only with the troops, but also with both junior and senior officers. Someone in Washington must have realized the low morale situation, because almost overnight more luxuries began to show up. All the items were consumables. Things such as candy, chips, and sundries began to be distributed to units on the front line on a regular basis. These were called sundry packs (SPs). The packages also contained cartons of cigarettes, small packets of cigars, toilet paper packs, as well as cans of fruit and juice. Prior to December, SPs were a rarity. During the previous period, January through November, seldom would these types of items be sent to a company. But it became apparent that the government was now attempting to buy off the men with small goodies, just like adults who pushed lollipops at small children to placate them. No one was fooled by the ploy, though. It only caused more resentment and worse morale. The government had stooped to "feel-good" measures. It was too little, too late.

DECEMBER 6, 1967
MORE DEATH

Sergeant Schriner, the platoon guide whose brother had drowned in the States in July, had returned to Alpha Company in early August. The Lieutenant observed that Schriner was never the same after his emergency leave. He seemed despondent. His peer, Staff Sergeant Collins, the second platoon sergeant from the Lieutenant's former platoon, also noticed how Schriner had become gun shy. He didn't fully engage in battles. There was little either Collins or the Lieutenant could do. The two men were talking one night and Sergeant Collins confided,

"Shriner's just cheating death at the moment. He's lost his effectiveness since his brother's death."

"I agree. He's depressed," the Lieutenant replied. "He's been part of Alpha Company since last January. He's a good man, and we don't want to lose him. Can you talk with him to see if you can help, sergeant?"

"Sure, I'll do that," Collins replied.

"Thanks, I appreciate whatever you can do."

"Yes, sir."

On December 6, shortly after the conversation with Staff Sergeant Collins and about four months after Schriner's return, the Lieutenant got word that Sergeant Schriner had been killed at the DMZ near Con Thien. He'd been hit by a huge piece of shrapnel that had slammed into his chest. Most men wore flak jackets, but many did not zip them up because they were so cumbersome. Schriner may have left his unzipped, which could have explained why he took the fatal chunk of shrapnel. Then, too, the zippers were easily damaged, which made it nearly impossible for a corpsman to unzip the front of the flak jackets when treating the wounded. Most everyone ignored the battalion commander's orders to keep them "zipped up and buttoned up."

On December 7, shortly after the report of Sergeant Schriner's death, a US helicopter was shot down, and Alpha Company had to destroy it with C-4 plastic explosives. After the casualties were removed, the chopper was blown up so that the enemy couldn't strip the downed helicopter's equipment. Sadly, there were no survivors from the crash. The Lieutenant thought the deaths would never end. The reports of KIAs flooded the radio traffic continuously.

DECEMBER 17, 1967
ANOTHER TRAGEDY

While listening to radio messages on December 17, the Lieutenant heard about the casualties from Alpha Company located near Con Thien.

"Staff Sergeant Collins, Alpha Company, has been killed at the DMZ by artillery fire," the radio operator's voice declared in a matter-of-fact tone.

The Lieutenant felt as if he'd been sucker-punched in the gut. Collins had been his platoon sergeant for seven months, and an extremely valuable member of the company since December 1966, about the same time as the Lieutenant reported for duty with Alpha Company.

No. Not Sergeant Collins. Surely, not him. He was so full of life. Everyone loved him. He can't be dead. He's one of our very best.

The incoming report indicated that Collins had been hit in the face by shrapnel, an identical wound to the one the Lieutenant had sustained in February. The only difference was that the fragment hitting Collins had gone just an inch higher, directly into his brain. He'd died instantly. The men wrapped him in a poncho, but Collins' body couldn't be evacuated for another three days, because the miserable weather prevented choppers from landing, and because of heavy NVA fire.

A hulk of a man, Collins was popular with all. He had a reputation in Company A far bigger than being the platoon sergeant of the Second Platoon. He was known for his fearlessness with a machine gun. He was remembered for storming the enemy bunker, firing as he went.

First Sergeant Crawford, who was there with Collins at the time, ensured that every man in the company could momentarily lay down his weapon and pay his respects and say his good-byes to Staff Sergeant Collins, as the gentle giant lay on the ground on the spot where he died. In solemn tribute, the men silently filed past the Marine's body while gunfire continued all around them. Somehow, this act seemed a fitting honor for the valiant warrior. The gesture was a rare, but heartfelt sign of respect for the beloved staff sergeant.

As a leader, he'd motivated men to do better than they thought they could. It wasn't just the men on the line who felt his loss; officers felt his death keenly as well. Captain Keith Thompson, his company commander, was just devastated by the news. So was the Lieutenant.

One time, the Lieutenant and Staff Sergeant Collins had a disagreement over promoting a man in the Second Platoon to become a squad leader. Collins was against the promotion. He felt the man wasn't qualified to lead. The Lieutenant, however, was for the promotion. In the end, the Lieutenant won, and the man in question proved himself a very capable leader. To Sergeant Collins' credit, he publicly stated that he'd been wrong and that the Lieutenant had been right. He gained even more status and respect in the Lieutenant's eyes for his admission, as well as in the eyes of the men in the platoon for his humility. All who knew him intensely felt his loss.

Collins thirteen-month tour was almost up. He had been due to rotate back to the States in a few of weeks, just before the Lieutenant. Staff Sergeant Collins never married and had no children. But he held the esteem of everyone he'd met in Vietnam.

One courageous warrior; ferocious, yet kind. One helluva excellent Marine. The best, really. Staff Sergeant Eugene Collins went home to Norfolk, Virginia, in a box.

CASHING IN BEER RATIONS

One positive advantage about being trapped in the rear was that each man was able to purchase rations for up to two cans of beer per day. The rations could be cashed in at the joint officer and staff NCO mess tent. Fortunately, there were some non-drinkers who freely sold their rations to anyone who wanted them. The Lieutenant and

First Sergeant Crawford managed to collect more than enough for a night of solid drinking.

Consequently, the Lieutenant sat in the mess tent furnished with tables and chairs and a few light bulbs dangling from the tent's square beams. The weather was cold, damp, and windy that night, and it was cold inside the mess tent, too. But the Lieutenant was relaxing with a beer at a table, along with First Sergeant Crawford. Both men were commiserating the losses of Staff Sergeant Collins and Sergeant Schriner.

After a few warm beers (they were never served cold), the Lieutenant confided to Crawford, "I want you to know how much I appreciate what you did for Staff Sergeant Collins in giving the men the chance to pay their respects, even under the most difficult of circumstances. I don't think we've done that over this last year for anyone else in Alpha Company. If anyone deserved the men's admiration, it surely was Collins."

"I realize it was dangerous there," Sergeant Crawford replied, "but I did what I did for the sake of the men, because they looked up to him for the courage they needed, especially during the times they were facing sure death." Crawford went on. "What makes this whole thing so damn frustrating is that both Collins and Schriner had less than thirty days to go after being in the thick of it for the last year."

"Yeah, that's what this stinkin' war does. You just don't know when your number will come up. They both almost made it. But 'almost' doesn't count here," the Lieutenant answered.

The two men continued talking about the war for some time, all the while drinking beer. Sergeant Crawford started talking some about his days in the Korean War.

The Lieutenant asked, "Were things as screwed up back then as they are now?"

"Just as frustrating back then as it is today, but we're the ones here to get the job done, and somehow we'll make it through," Crawford said.

"Yeah, I guess we will, somehow."

The Lieutenant and Sergeant Crawford kept drinking for a while longer. Late into the night when they decided to leave, First Sergeant Crawford, a big and tall man who outweighed the Lieutenant by a good bit, attempted to stand. Unfortunately, he had become so snockered that he could barely walk. The Lieutenant, himself unsteady on his feet, attempted to half carry the first sergeant back to his tent. The two were a ridiculous sight—both drunk and staggering into the night. It was hard to tell which one was holding up the other. Fortunately, the area was quiet, and no one saw them.

They grieved their losses together that night, which helped some, but the next morning, the Lieutenant's head hurt like crazy, and his mouth felt like it was stuffed with cotton. After only a few hours sleep, he lay on his cot and stared absently into space.

DEPRESSION

The months of frustration and anger, along with feelings of hopelessness and intense loss, engulfed the Lieutenant like an old wet coat. He felt as if the only solution to his misery was going home, yet he already knew somehow that home wouldn't be the same either. He didn't have the answer. He could no longer clearly see his way forward. He felt as though he'd been frozen in time while the world as he once knew it had changed dramatically. Equally, the Lieutenant felt he had changed radically but didn't understand what it was that he had changed from, or what he had changed into. He had no idea how to process the change. What was frightening was the future—not knowing how the unknown changes would affect him once he returned home—if he made it home alive. It was as if he was losing all sense of reality. *Can't go back, can't go forward, can't stay where I am.*

His mind often wandered. He stayed alone, enveloped in a dark place inside himself. He drifted through routine days and lay awake nights. Losing himself in booze became his only relief—and that didn't happen nearly often enough because of his lack of access to the glorious painkiller. Worse, he began to feel he no longer belonged anywhere.

I relate to the enlisted men, because just a year ago I was a corporal, E-4, plucked from obscurity to become an officer. But I don't really belong with them anymore. I don't fit in with the senior NCOs either, because they have the experience I don't. And I really can't relate to the college guys who are lieutenants. They have the education I wish I had. I just feel like a corporal impersonating a lieutenant. I don't belong anywhere anymore. I'm a misfit.

The Lieutenant, who generally didn't have much to say unless it was necessary, withdrew further. If anyone noticed, they didn't tell him. He kept his thoughts to himself while he spent the final days of December slogging through the humdrum of after-action reports, situation reports, and command chronologies.

DECEMBER 24, 1967
REMEMBERING THE LAST YEAR

Just before Christmas, the Lieutenant's wife mailed him an eighteen-inch-high artificial Christmas tree, a pathetic-looking thing, along with a box of cheap ornaments. He donated it to the mess tent so everyone could see something familiar from home. Propped on a table in a corner, it was the only seasonal decoration.

It was questionable whether anyone appreciated it or not, but he didn't much care. Along with the tree, his wife also sent a fifth of Wild Turkey whiskey, a gift that he appreciated much more than the tree. He knew he would drown his sorrows in the booze as soon as he was off duty. Whenever a bottle of whiskey showed up in any junior officer's the mail, a rare thing, friends gathered around eagerly, and the bottle got passed around for everyone to enjoy a swig. Everyone had "friends" when hard liquor appeared. Eventually, the other officers who had come to take a pull on the whiskey bottle wandered off.

Late at night, the Lieutenant sat on the edge of his cot, drinking from the bottle and thinking.

This is my second consecutive Christmas away from home. Couldn't they cut us some slack and let us go home a few weeks early? Last year at this time, I was sitting in Okinawa waiting to be assigned to a company. Why can't I get an early out so I can get home for the holidays? I know others who feel this way, too. It would sure boost morale to only miss one Christmas instead of two.

He'd left home on the fifth of December last year. He and his wife had stayed up all night talking and just being together. At dawn the next morning, he packed his seabag and changed into his uniform. He didn't want her to go to the airport to see him off for his flight to San Diego, because he couldn't stand the idea of a teary airport farewell. He wanted to remember her at home in their little apartment. So there she stayed.

A few hours later when his plane landed in San Diego, he was bussed to Camp Pendleton, California, where he spent two weeks waiting for a flight out of the country. During that time, he was assigned duty as the payroll officer. He carried an ammo can around with about $20,000 cash inside it to pay the troops stationed there. He was also assigned visiting duty for Marines in the brig. It felt like wasted time. He only wanted to begin ticking off the days until his return. The time in California hadn't counted against his thirteen-month tour of duty. He couldn't begin counting the days until he arrived in Okinawa almost three weeks later, which put him there on Christmas Eve, 1966. That was one year ago, to the day.

He had no sooner reported for duty last year, when as a Christmas gift, the Lieutenant's new battalion commander, Lieutenant Colonel "Blackjack" Westerman, in a spirit of generosity, gave each of his officers the December issue of Playboy magazine. Westerman, a crusty old Marine, was a favorite commanding officer of some, but the Lieutenant was unimpressed. He'd never been one for girly magazines.

By New Year's Eve 1966, he had already taken up his assignment as Weapons Platoon commander. New men had joined the company recently. Some came directly from the States and were being integrated into Alpha Company. Others, who had already seen combat, were temporally transported from Vietnam back to Okinawa via ship for reassignment to different platoons. Alpha Company was ordered to move to a training area in northern Okinawa for tactical operations in order to integrate all new arrivals. In February, the company sailed for Vietnam.

The entire year of 1967 has been for nothing. A stupid, pointless war against "communist aggression." A failure. All bullshit. This is hard to figure out from where I am.

Then his thoughts shifted to more personal matters.

I've missed every major holiday and most of the important celebrations of my first year and a half of marriage. I'm bitter. At least this damn war has given me the opportunity to make something of myself. I'm drawing a half-decent paycheck, with combat pay to boot. Officers pay sure beats what I made as a corporal. Maybe someday I'll be an old man, sitting in a rocking chair, telling half-true war stories. Or maybe I'll be an old man in a funny hat, walking in a parade honoring veterans. But the Lieutenant didn't like that idea any better than sitting in a rocking chair. *What a price we've paid.*

The Lieutenant tipped the bottle up and polished off the rest of his wife's gift like a dehydrated man drinks water. As he'd neared the end of his tour, drinking had become the only relief for his wounded soul. But booze only temporarily dulled the pain he was determined not to feel.

CHAPTER 16

LETTER FROM HOME

JANUARY 18, 1968

January was as dismal and boring as December had been. The days crept by at a maddeningly slow pace. Ticking them off one by one on his calendar just about drove the Lieutenant crazy. In fact, he wondered if he still had any sanity.

He received a letter from his wife two days before he was due to begin processing out. He knew other letters she had written would be returned to the States.

January 12, 1968

My darling,

It seems as if I have been remiss in the matter of handling our money. My dad dropped in the other day and asked me if I was all ready for you to come home. I said yes and he asked, "Well, do you have all your finances in order?"

So I said, "I guess." Then he asked if I had all my bank statements reconciled. I had no idea what he was talking about, so I just said, "What?" He said, "You know, when you get your cancelled checks in the mail from the bank each month. What do you do with them?"

"Well, I know you're supposed to save them, so I throw them in the desk drawer with all the others."

My dad said, "You mean you've been putting them in the drawer for a whole year and you've never opened them?"

"Yeah."

He slapped his forehead, like I was dumb or something. Then he asked if he could see my checkbook and the old statements to be sure we had enough money in our account. He spent the next several hours going over all our statements. In the end, our checkbook was ten cents off. I don't think that's any big deal, but he said it drove him nuts trying to find the lost dime.

Who cares about ten cents? I knew all along we had enough money, because I hardly ever spend any. I wasn't worried one little bit. Anyway, I'm glad you'll be home soon to take over all this bank stuff.

Remember how much I love you and miss you. Come home to me and our baby soon. I can't wait 'til you're really here. Sending kisses across the miles.

Your loving wife

The Lieutenant just chuckled and shook his head.

JANUARY 19, 1968
HEADING HOME

The Lieutenant's last day. From his C-2 bunker, mid-way between Cam Lo and Con Thien, he could hear and feel the steady thundering and reverberations of heavy artillery in the distance. Occasionally, incoming rounds hit nearby.

He walked around shaking hands and saying his goodbyes to the remaining men of Company A who had been with him from January through August, the period when he'd served as platoon commander and executive officer. The Lieutenant felt intensely emotional saying goodbye, knowing "his" men still had months of fighting, pain, and the ever-present threat of death ahead of them.

"Just want to say goodbye and wish you all the best. Stay alert," the Lieutenant cautioned.

"Goodbye, sir, and best of luck to you." The words were heartfelt from all.

"Thank you. It's been an honor to serve with you," he told each man. He meant it, too. He felt privileged to have served with these courageous, bold, and daring Marines.

Saying goodbye to the S-3 staff was easier, more pro-forma. The Lieutenant knew the 3A assignment had been far better than counting the "socks and jocks" in some supply warehouse. He felt grateful he hadn't been assigned elsewhere, but still, it was a job he'd rather not have had. Commanding his platoon had always been his preference, even under combat conditions.

After checking with the S-4 (logistics) about getting a ride to Dong Ha, a corpsman volunteered, "There's an ambulance heading back to Dong Ha. There're no wounded in it, and the docs won't mind. You can hitch a ride in it."

So the Lieutenant climbed in the back where wooden benches lined either side of the truck, and rode sideways in silence for about forty-five minutes or so. The ambulance had a big white circle, like a bulls-eye, with a red cross painted in the middle on both sides of the truck. He wondered if he had become a moving target. The enemy was known to attack any emergency or life-rescue vehicle. Ambulances were no exception. The ride was uneventful, though.

REFLECTION

Dong Ha was his processing out point for the battalion. From there, he caught a huge C-130 plane headed south to Da Nang. Sitting in the cargo hold, the noise from the plane's gigantic engines rattled his nerves. He felt restless and jittery, but thankfully, the flight was relatively short. For two days he endured further out-processing, including a standard medical exam and endless paperwork, but mostly just sitting on a bunk, waiting for news of his next flight out.

During his wait in Da Nang, the Lieutenant was billeted in an area reserved strictly for guys heading home. About thirty officers were grouped in one large sleeping building built of plywood and screens and lined inside with cots. At night, he could hear guys waking up. Some screamed or cried out; a reaction to combat withdrawal. This was something the Lieutenant feared might happen to him. Some men sat on their bunks shaking. The Lieutenant found the whole experience unnerving. It reminded him of the night on R&R in Hawaii, when he fell off the bed thinking he was rolling into a foxhole yelling about 106 incoming. He didn't like to think about firepower and how it damaged and distorted human beings. Instead he told himself, *I will harden my heart against every bit of war. I will not let any of what I've seen or experienced get to me. I won't think about it, and I won't talk about it. I will only look forward, not backwards.*

Finally, the men received word that they would be flown out around noon the following day, January 21. No one slept that night, and no one left the hut, just in case there was a flight change.

On the next the leg of his trip he flew in a 707 from Da Nang to Okinawa's Kadena Air Force Base, a trip of well over nine hours. On that flight, there was nothing much to do but think. Guys didn't talk to one another at all. Neither did the Lieutenant speak with anyone. Men just kept their thoughts to themselves and listened only to the voices inside their own heads.

Why am I alive while so many others are now dead? Why me? How come I survived? Why do I deserve to live? Someone said this feeling is called 'survivor's guilt.' Now I understand why.

These thoughts haunted him throughout the flights home. Every time the Lieutenant closed his eyes, he could see the faces of the men who had died, and he named their names: PFC Huckleberry, PFC Johnson, Corporals Jacob, Jack Wolpe, Agar, and Greene; Sergeants

Schriner, Gustafson, Amos, and Collins; Lieutenants Biff Mullins, Jackson Cox, Dick Roush, Chuck Lamson, Bill Roach, John Poole; and the list went on.

As the parade of fighting brothers faces marched through his head, he forced himself to stop thinking of them by name. *I have to stop naming them. The list is too long. I need to stop. I feel so proud to have served with them. All of them too young to die. God help us!*

Then he pictured the widows and parents back home, standing over the flag-draped coffins of their loved ones. Women sobbing. The burial details. "Taps" playing. All the little kids who didn't understand and who wouldn't ever know their fathers.

He thought back to the very first person he'd learned about who had been killed in Vietnam. It happened in April 1965, not long after the Lieutenant (then a lance corporal) finished boot camp, and while he still lived at the Marine barracks in Jacksonville. His commanding officer chose nineteen Marines for burial detail for a killed-in-action Marine corporal whose hometown was Live Oak, Florida. Jacksonville was the nearest Marine unit to Live Oak.

Ten men carried rifles for the three-gun volley salute to be fired honoring the fallen man just before the Marine bugler played "Taps." Additionally six pallbearers, one NCO in charge, and the bus driver, Sergeant Merwin, completed the detail. It was July, and wearing their wool dress blue uniforms in the extreme Florida humidity made the Marines drip sweat like fast-melting ice. The stifling heat made it hard to breathe. The Lieutenant, who, at that time, had attained the enlisted rank of lance corporal, was chosen to be a pallbearer.

The official gray government bus arrived at the little dilapidated church right on time. The place was packed. The deceased Marine was already there at the front of the church, laid out in his coffin, arrayed in full dress blues. The Marine detail marched up the center aisle to the seats reserved for them on the left side and filed into the first three pews in perfect formation.

When the Baptist minister stepped up to the pulpit, no one had any indication that he would pontificate there in the heat for well over an hour. He was full of fire and emotion, and he let it rip full throttle to all within earshot. The Lieutenant really didn't pay that much attention to what was being said. He was fascinated with being in a plain church setting with hard wooden pews. Robed choir members sat behind the pulpit. He was accustomed to seeing a Catholic altar with a crucifix behind it. He moved his eyes as far as he dared without turning his head, so he could take in his surroundings. Women fluttered round paper fans with the funeral home logo printed on them, trying to catch a little breeze in the heat. The church had no air-conditioning, or even an overhead fan. The stained glass windows were various colors but without pictures. Yet, his eyes kept riveting to the coffin in front of him.

After the preaching was over, the minister invited the congregation to file past the coffin for one last look at the deceased. Some of the mourners lined up for a second look. The parade around the room continued until the preacher called out,

"No seconds, brothers and sisters, no seconds!"

Everyone's clothes stuck to the pews and peeled away from the wooden benches, leaving wet marks behind them when they stood. The Marines kept sweating. Regrettably, the service lasted for well over two hours, while the Marine contingent sat sweltering at ramrod attention in the front rows.

Before they got on the bus to drive to the graveyard, the funeral director let the men know that the young Marine who was about to be buried, a Marine who had given his life serving his country, could not be buried in the Live Oak National Cemetery. The reason given was that cemetery was located inside the Live Oak city limits. A city ordinance forbad Negroes from being buried inside city limits.

As if anyone would look inside the coffin to see his black skin! How stupid! When a comrade in arms falls dead on the battlefield, his blood runs out the same color red as anyone else's. Marines fight side by side, and we die side by side. There's no discrimination about who gets killed. He was one of us, a US Marine. What good was there in a segregated cemetery? Damn! What a crazy world.

Following the hearse, the bus drove to an old, ill-kept grave-yard with weeds that grew waste high. There, the Leatherneck pall-bearers carried the casket through the abundant overgrowth to the freshly dug grave, where they laid their fellow Marine to rest. After the gun salute by the riflemen and the playing of "Taps," the flag was folded perfectly by six white-gloved hands. The senior NCO presented the flag to the next of kin, the Marine's parents, with con-dolences on behalf of the United States Marine Corps.

Still in flight, the Lieutenant shifted in his seat, lit another ciga-rette, and settled back into his thoughts once again. He asked him-self, *how many times since that day has the same scene been repeated at burials?* The answer he didn't want to hear was, *tens of thousands.*

After the cemetery, immediately following the burial, the men on the bus were hungry. They hadn't eaten since breakfast, and it was approaching five o'clock. The NCO in charge okayed opting for the nearest café in the small town square. The Marines filed out of the bus, impatient for any kind of grub. About half of the men were black, the other half white. Some of the Marines sat at the counter on stools and some sat at the little square tables for four.

A gnarly, gray-haired white woman behind the counter made no bones about the fact that she didn't want to serve the group because some were black. Possibly in agreement with her, all the other patrons got up from their chairs and left the café en masse. But because the Leathernecks were all in uniform, and because they were a party of nineteen paying customers, she finally relented and served the Marines. She made a point, though, of slamming the plates in front of the black Marines. To add offense to an already bad situation, while the Marines ate, a crowd of about forty or so white townsmen gathered outside. They stared through the plate-glass window watching the men like caged animals at the zoo. The Marines ate in silence, but since a large mirror was mounted on the wall behind the counter, they all could see everything that was happening outside. One obnoxious man, obviously the ringleader, kept yanking the screen door open, sticking only his head inside the door, and shouting racial epithets, before slamming the door shut again.

Quietly, the Marines formed a plan. With typical twenty-year-old mentality, they decided they'd bolt for the bus and grab the rifles they had used for the salute to the fallen Marine. Then they'd fix bayonets, for they had used up the ammunition issued to them, and go for an all-out brawl, breaking as many redneck heads as they could. Those without weapons could use fists. That would surely teach those local yahoo bastards a lesson.

They were all in, including four black Marines from California and two from New York. However, the three Negro Marines who hailed from the South persuaded the rest not to follow such a plan of action.

"If we start any trouble, I promise you, there will be lynchings and house burnings for the next two weeks," the tallest of the three advised. "Let's keep our cool, get back on the bus, and get the hell outta here."

In the end, that's exactly what the Marines did.

The Lieutenant still felt badly for the loved ones of that young Marine from Live Oak, Florida. In his mind, they had received the ultimate insult after their son's service to his country.

JANUARY 23, 1968
OKINAWA: MORE OUT-PROCESSING

Finally, "wheels down" at Kadena Airfield, Okinawa. They were officially out of the war zone. No incoming, no snipers, no gunfire, no artillery. There was almost an eerie quiet all around them. It seemed overwhelming to grasp such a strange new reality.

At nearby Camp Hanson, the Lieutenant traded his utility uniform for a class-A uniform consisting of dull-green wool trousers and coat, khaki shirt and tie, and a garrison cap. He sat for almost three days waiting to be processed out. During the interminable wait, the Lieutenant purchased himself a snappy three-piece suit at the PX, which was ostensibly "tailor-made." It was a bargain price. Besides, he needed a good suit. The Lieutenant folded the new suit carefully and stuffed it in his already full seabag. He also bought cigarettes and a few snacks for the long plane ride home.

Later, he strolled into the bar at the officer's club and encountered a former classmate from The Basic School, Jack Francis, now also a first lieutenant. But Jack was a wreck and nearly inconsolable. The day before, Jack had gotten shit-faced, passed out, and missed his flight home. He'd had no choice but to wait for a vacancy on an outbound flight. That could take a few more days. So there he sat at the bar, drinking away his sorrows. The two of them had a drink together, then another.

CHAPTER 17

USA, HERE I COME

JANUARY 27, 1968

Every passenger on the World Airways 707 jet out of Kadena Air
Force Base, Okinawa, was a serviceman headed for one destination only: the good old US of A. Kadena to Marine Air Station at
El Toro in California was the longest leg of the trip home. Tickets
home on World Airways were issued individually as part of out-processing. World Airways was a marginally safe, no-name airline company that the government used to ferry troops over and back from
the States. The Marines dubbed it "Daisy Duck Airlines" because
no one had ever heard of it.

I just hope the damn thing makes it over the Pacific in one piece.

He kept his thoughts to himself, as did his seatmate. In fact, it
seemed as if none of the other passengers spoke during the trip,
either. The planeload of returning servicemen was just too quiet.
The Lieutenant tried to snooze on the long flight, but it was hot
and cramped, and his thoughts got all jumbled up in his head. He
chain-smoked. His head was pounding and so was his jaw. He went
from disbelief at going home to euphoria, from profound sadness to

elation. As the eleven-hour flight dragged on, he relived battles that he'd fought, then tried hard to forget them.

Just think about home, he told himself. *Try to picture her face when she greets you.*

But death kept taking precedence over his thoughts.

Why didn't I die like I should have? He asked himself for the millionth time. *Sometimes it seemed like everyone who served died. As young men, we're supposed to think we're invincible, but any Marine who has been to battle knows that isn't the truth. Every day teenage boys and young men are still dying horrible deaths. They lie bloody and dirty and dead on the orange clay ground, sprawled in either dust or mud in a foreign land, their bodies torn apart like rag dolls that the dog chewed. Forever gone, only a memory. Why did I live?*

The words from church echoed in his head: "Remember, man, you are dust, and to dust you shall return." That's what the priest said when he put black ashes on your forehead at the start of Lent. Those words kept reverberating in his brain.

He wondered about his future. He now had orders to train new second lieutenants at Quantico, Virginia, at The Basic School.

What will that be like? I wonder how I can ever earn a college degree. I'll need one if I stay in the Corps. It's something I'd better look into. I won't get a promotion past captain if I don't get some education. That might be tricky, though.

Yet, more than anything, he couldn't bring himself to think about returning to Southeast Asia. He simply prayed that the wretched war would be over before his two-year turnaround time came again.

ON US SOIL

After deplaning at Marine Air Station, El Toro, in California, the Lieutenant, along with three other returning lieutenants, grabbed a cab for the hour-long ride to the Los Angeles Airport. The Lieutenant slightly knew two of the guys from The Basic School. At LAX, they disbursed in different directions like fleeing captives, each eager to catch his own flight home. Since they had crossed the International Date Line, the date was still January 27.

The Lieutenant wove his way through the airport crowd, eyes searching for signs to his gate.

Maybe I'll get lucky enough to catch an earlier flight home, he hoped.

FROM OUT OF THE CROWD

While walking through a congested concourse, he noticed coming toward him a tall, hollow-eyed, very gaunt, young army sergeant with his duffle bag on one shoulder. The man stuck out because he was at least a head taller than most of the mob of people in the airport. He wore a deer-in-the-headlights look that said *I'm going home*. When they came to within several meters of one another, the Lieutenant wondered if he had that same look about himself.

Suddenly, from out of the throng of people came a scruffy, long-haired kid wearing blue jeans and a tie-dyed T-shirt. He lunged toward the sergeant from the crowd, as if from nowhere. From the Lieutenant's vantage point, he could see the boy staring at the sergeant with hate in his eyes. The boy then hurled a great wad of spit onto the sergeant, and just as quickly, the assailant sprinted away. The sergeant stopped and stood there, stunned. A bewildered expression instantly came over his face. Spittle dripped down the combat ribbons affixed to his uniform breast.

The Lieutenant stared after the kid, speechless. For a moment, he considered chasing after the hippie before he realized there was no point trying to race after the culprit. He was long gone. The sergeant regained his composure, wiped the spittle off his uniform with his handkerchief, and continued walking.

The little jerk, the Lieutenant thought. *What a mean, random act. Probably some cowardly, draft-dodging bastard.*

Both servicemen kept walking, and only acknowledged one another as they passed with quick salutes, as military etiquette required.

From his time spent away, the Lieutenant had only a small inkling of the growing political unrest in the States. Try as he did, he couldn't make any sense of the incident.

ALMOST HOME

Still feeling unsettled by the spitting incident, the Lieutenant located his gate and ducked into a phone booth to call his wife, collect.

"I'm in LA. I'm trying to get an earlier flight out!" he exclaimed.

"Which airport? I'll be there!"

"Not sure, but I'll be home in just a few hours! I'll call you as soon as I land."

He managed to catch an earlier flight into Dulles Airport. On the cross–country plane ride home, he thought about the time when he'd been stationed in Jacksonville, early on, when he had received orders to go to Vietnam. It was sometime in late 1965, and several others from his barracks had received those same orders. At the last minute though, the Lieutenant's orders were rescinded and he was sent to Officer Candidate School instead. Later, he heard on the news that this same group from his barracks, along with other Marines, had died. They had flown out from El Toro Marine Corps Base in California, but their airplane stalled on take-off and had crashed into a mountainside, killing all on board. That would be the first of his many close calls during his wartime experience.

Why was I chosen to live? The nagging in his head wouldn't stop. The closer he got to home, the more his anxiety built.

Is this plane going to crash, too? Why can't it go any faster? He tried to sleep, but he was too exhausted and overcome with emotion—so much emotion. He lit another cigarette and thought about his thirteen months of duty in the hellhole called Vietnam.

It's been quite a year. I can't go back in time and change a thing. I desperately wish I could. My thoughts have unwillingly become captive to this war. I'm a prisoner in my own head.

As his flight neared the East Coast, the Lieutenant admitted to himself that he wasn't the same person who had left home thirteen months earlier.

I'm hard and callous now. It was the only way to survive the war. He wished he could just shove all the death and carnage from his time away inside a closed box somewhere far in the back of his mind and forget about it. But the thoughts of war just wouldn't go away. He forced himself back to the present.

Will she notice that I've changed? Does she still love me? Or has my absence made her grow unsure? Will she accept me for who I've become? What's it gonna be like living in a house with a baby and a wife? And plumbing! Will I get used to sleeping on a real bed again? Will I ever adjust to a regular life?

It seemed too good to be true that he was really going home. He could hardly believe it. He just wanted to get off the plane.

AT LAST

He never bothered to call her when he landed. Instead, he dashed curbside and hailed a cab. When he gave the address to the driver, he added, "Step on it, please! I'm in a big hurry!"

The ride from the airport took about forty-five minutes. When he finally arrived at his apartment building around eight o'clock that night, he bounded through the front door, pressed the number four on the elevator then raced to the end of the hall to their apartment, number 404. Taking a deep breath, he dropped his seabag with a heavy thud, and knocked. Almost immediately, his wife threw the door open. They stood there on the threshold, locked in each other's arms, for a long, long time.

Finally, she took his hand and said softly, "Come and meet your son."

EPILOGUE

Two and a half years later, as his tour of duty in Quantico was coming to an end, the Lieutenant, by then a Captain, was unenthusiastically anticipating new orders for a second tour of duty in Vietnam. He expected the orders to arrive any day.

On a balmy evening in the spring of 1970, he spent an enjoyable night out with his wife at some official social function on the base. Wearing his dress blue uniform, he escorted his heavily pregnant wife to the event. On their way home, they decided on a whim to stop in for a quick nightcap at the bachelor officers quarters bar located inside Liversedge Hall. His wife called the babysitter from the club phone booth in the lobby to ensure all was okay, and then they sauntered into the bar.

Every cushy seat was taken around the low, round cocktail tables. The place was crowded, mostly with junior officers and their dates. The only spots available in the smoky room were two side-by-side stools at the bar. Behind the bar, a large mirror ran its length, with rows of liquor bottles lined up on the counter in front.

The Captain gently helped his wife onto one of the stools. As he took the seat to her right, he looked into the mirror, and in a flash, he swiveled around and jumped off his stool. He landed behind his dumbfounded wife at the same time as the man who had been sitting on her left flew off his stool.

The two men grabbed one another by the shoulders. They jumped and danced in circles, all the while yelling and whooping. For several minutes, they yipped their delight with the joyful glee of children.

Normally quiet and proper, the Captain had completely abandoned all decorum. His wife had never seen her husband show this much boisterous emotion.

Every conversation in the place came to a dead stop. Every eye in the room focused on the two twirling men. The entire bar grew eerily quiet. Even the jukebox noise wailing in the distance seemed to grow faint.

"Man, I thought you were dead!" Captain John Moffett shouted in disbelief at the Captain.

"And I thought *you* were dead!" came the elated reply.

The two Marines warmly embraced. Both men had been wounded in Vietnam two years earlier. Both men had seen the other's name on a casualty report list that hadn't distinguished between killed in action or wounded in action. Each assumed the other had been killed. They had trained together at Officer Candidate School and The Basic School in the same class. Both men were mustangs. They were absolutely elated to see each other alive and well.

After all the death, destruction, heartbreak, and loss, here—at last—was one very good outcome, an outcome truly worthy of celebrating.

POSTSCRIPT

The Lieutenant returned to Vietnam for a second one-year tour in December 1970, with the rank of captain. This time his assignment was as a Marine advisor to the Vietnamese Marines. During his second tour there, he fully realized how poorly the US had prepared the Vietnamese for conventional war. The South Vietnamese had become so dependent on US tactics, air support, and logistics that they could not stand on their own. The Captain believed the Americans were fighting a losing battle. By the end of his second tour, he more fully resented US politicians in general. He blamed them for ineptitude in both the military and political leadership of the war in Vietnam.

For ten years after his first tour of duty in Vietnam, he brooded. He seethed inwardly and he drank heavily. He couldn't come to terms with the terrible loss of life. He couldn't reconcile, rationalize, explain, or understand the ignorance and stupidity of that war. He selfishly looked into himself and never considered the impact of his depression on his wife and children.

By 1974, his wife found a new faith in Jesus. Her life changed dramatically, and the Lieutenant observed a new hope within her.

Perhaps, he thought, *I need that same kind of change. Does she have what I'm so desperately searching for?*

He reexamined his life. It was a mess. How could the world culture he knew from the past so radically have changed in such a short time? He knew there had to be something more to life. He searched, yet he couldn't find any answers. But he continued to notice the change for good in his wife over the next three years.

Finally, in 1977, the Captain came to the end of himself. He considered his lack of faith in God and realized he wanted whatever it was his wife had. He needed the same kind of faith in Jesus that she experienced. He asked her to pray for him. Instead, she responded, "You have to make the prayer yourself."

He confessed his sins and sought forgiveness and gave his heart to Jesus Christ. In doing this, he was able to relinquish control of the confused tangle of anger and resentment he still held onto from his war experiences. As he began to trust Jesus with his entire being, as he yielded to biblical teachings, he found that he no longer needed the crutches he had used in the past. He had found peace at last. And he knew deep down that the peace was real. He was set free!

From that time on, he kept the little Bible on the corner of his desk that Sergeant Gottlieb had sent to him while he was still in Vietnam. The Captain willingly shared his new beliefs with anyone who was curious about his conversion. That Bible remained on whatever desk he occupied while he completed his twenty-year career in the Marine Corps.

He finished college in 1975, majoring in history. While still on active duty, he obtained two master's degrees. In 1984, after he retired from the Marine Corps, he began a new career in business. In 2004, he retired again.

By then in his sixties, he attended seminary, earned a Master of Divinity degree and eventually a Doctor of Ministry degree. In the interim, he was ordained a minister in the Anglican Communion, and began a church that catered to the elderly and those suffering from Alzheimer's disease. He continued to share the gospel of Jesus

Christ with anyone who would listen. He believed that God had kept him alive during both of his Vietnam tours for a reason.

In his calling, he pastored, preached the gospel, and cared for the elderly, sick, and dying in the States. He'd found his niche. He still tried to forget the war that did not take him, but knew those gruesome memories would always be with him.

He and his wife became the proud parents of three loving children, and eventually celebrated more than fifty years of marriage.

In conclusion, he could wholeheartedly proclaim along with the modern day songwriter and Paul's Epistle to the Romans, "I'm no longer a slave to fear; I am a child of God." (Romans 8:15, New American Standard Bible)

GLOSSARY

amtrac: amphibious tractor

ARVN: Army of the Republic of South Vietnam

The Basic School: officer basic training at Quantico following Officer Candidate School

battalion landing team (BLT): composite force of an infantry battalion, a tank platoon, a company of amphibious tractors, a shore party platoon, a motor transport section, a logistics support unit detachment, an engineer platoon, a reconnaissance detachment, scouts and snipers detachment, and a medical platoon

bazookas: slang for a 3.5-inch rocket launcher (weapon)

BOQ: bachelor officers quarters

brig: military word for "jail"

brown bar: second lieutenant

casualty call: personal Headquarters Marine Corps representative notifying the next of kin of Marine suffering a casualty, death, or wounding

Claymore mines: portable explosive device detonated by wire from a distance

COC: combat operations center

C-rations: combat food, in a box

C-2: defensive location between Con Thien and Cam Lo

C-4: a plastic explosive

DMZ: demilitarized zone, geographical area between North and South Vietnam

dog tags: metal embossed identification worn around the neck by all personnel

duffle bag: army term for a large green canvas bag for a soldier's clothing

fix bayonets: removing a knife-like object from its sheath and fixing it to the end of the rifle as if using a spear point

garrison cap: long and narrow-shaped uniform cover (hat) worn for less formal occasions

gunny: gunnery sergeant

I Corps: northeastern section of South Vietnam, including the demilitarized zone

KIA: killed in action

Mattel: brand name of a US toy maker

mechanical mules: a four-wheeled motorized vehicle with a flat-bed much like a very large wagon

medivac: medical evacuation

mess: dining hall, in Vietnam, a large general-purpose tent

NCO: non-commissioned officer

NVA: North Vietnamese Army, the enemy

OCS: Officer Candidate School

old man: any superior officer

ordnance: ammunition, bombs, artillery, or any explosive device or weapon

perimeter: circular defense position that can be either permanent or temporary

pogue: a staff officer or enlisted man who stays in the rear and out of the line of fire

poncho: rubberized knee-length square rain-covering with a hole in the middle for one's head

PRC: prefix for radios, e.g., PRC—6, PRC—10, PRC—25; often pronounced "prick"

Purple Heart: military medal awarded in the name of the president to anyone wounded or killed in battle while serving with the US military

PX: post exchange; store where basic dry goods and sundry items can be purchased while on a military installation

Quonset hut: semi-circular metal structure for housing or administrative use

R&R: rest and relaxation; each man was granted a one-week R&R leave during their tour of duty in Vietnam

recon: reconnaissance

RPG rockets: smaller version of a 3.5mm rocket (weapon)

Saigon: former capital city of South Vietnam

seabag: green canvas bag used by Navy and Marines to hold clothing, often carried on the shoulder

shelter half: devised in WWII; half of a pup tent carried by each man

Silver Star: medal awarded for extraordinary bravery in battle; third highest award after the Navy Cross and the Medal of Honor

SOP: standing operating procedure(s)

S-1: staff at battalion and regimental level; admin at division level is G 1-4 (general staff)

S-2: intelligence; a staff position

S-3: operations; a staff position

S-3A: assistant S-3

S-4: logistics; a staff position

S-5: civil affairs

slit trench: a narrow trench about a foot wide, perhaps five feet long, for human waste

tank: large tracked vehicle with machine gun and large gun capability

utilities: a green, standard-issue battle uniform

WIA: wounded in action

willy peter bag, or WP bag: (waterproof) a rubber waterproof bag, with a tie band used to store small items